FAVOURITE
ASSEMBLIES
FOR AGES 7-11

Edited by Anne Stewart OBE

pfp

© 2002 pfp publishing limited

First published in this form in Britain in 2002 by
pfp publishing limited
61 Gray's Inn Road
London WC1X 8TH

Reprinted 2002
Reprinted 2003

Written by Gerald Haigh.
Illustrations by Sue Wollatt of GCI, Pat Murray of GCI, Angela Lumley.
Cover and layout by Creative Media.
Cover photo by CD Vision.
Page design by Starfish Design for Print.

Other assembly titles available from pfp include
• *Favourite Assemblies for Ages 4–7*
• *Assemblies for Sensitive Issues*
• *The Primary Assembly Song Book*
• *All Year Round – Assemblies for Special Days and Celebrations*
• *Primary Assembly File*

pfp orders and customer service
Tel: 0870 241 0731

Printed in the UK

ISBN 1 874050 56 2

A catalogue record for this book is available from the British Library.

CONTENTS

INTRODUCTION

The 40 assemblies in this collection have been carefully selected by Anne Stewart OBE for use with older children aged between 7 and 11 years and are divided into the following common primary assembly themes.

- Abilities and achievements
- Differences and respecting others
- Myself
- How do I feel about that?
- My family
- Community and belonging
- Change
- Teamwork
- Thinking of others
- Awe and wonder

Taken from the *Primary Assembly File* subscription – a termly publication providing 60 brand new assemblies every year – these assemblies are the very best, all-time favourites from the entire collection.

Using the assemblies

Our assembly books are intended to support busy headteachers and teachers. They do this by providing you with assemblies which

- are easy to use
- tell stories that young children can enjoy
- carry serious spiritual messages.

You can use the assemblies in this book exactly as they are with very little preparation. Or, if you do have the time, then even a few minutes of preparation will make you more confident and allow you to adapt them to your own particular needs.

Good prior knowledge of an assembly means that you can

- pause for questions or discussion
- use poetry that you have chosen
- use children's writing or artwork
- set up simple role plays
- use periods of reflective silence
- tell the story in your own words
- edit the whole assembly for length or emphasis.

Each assembly begins with an introduction which leads into the main theme. Extra resources are clearly listed and only include items that are readily available in school.

The core of each assembly is a story or poem. These are self-contained and you can easily use them on their own, incorporating them into your own way of working. This is specially helpful in schools where the time available for assembly is very short.

Links to Bible stories are made where appropriate and those who prefer a stronger Christian approach find that they can build our stories into daily acts of worship. Finally, each assembly finishes with a prayer or a thought and some song suggestions.

However you use them, you will find that these assemblies are stimulating, well written and valuable and that they work with the children in your school.

Inventions

Assembly 1 of 4

This is about an invention that will make a big difference to many lives in the developing world. It reminds us that we depend on human ingenuity for so much, and that we are all capable of having bright ideas.

You will need

- a blank OHT and pens

- a few small gadgets ('inventions'), eg. can opener, pencil sharpener (go for things that are easy to understand rather than 'black box' electronics).

Taken by ....

Date ....

Given to ....

Comments

- ....

- ....

- ....

✦ Introduction

Hold up the gadgets.

What are these things?

Let the children name them.

On the OHT write: All of these gadgets were ……… by somebody.

What is the missing word?

Take suggestions. They may include 'made' and 'designed'.

If the word 'invented' is mentioned say:

That is a good word.

If the word 'invented' isn't mentioned say:

How about the word 'invented'?

What does 'invented' mean?

Take suggestions if there are any.

It means that somebody thought up the idea.

And what do you call a person who invents things? *Take suggestions.* An inventor.

Sometimes an inventor becomes famous.

Can anybody name some famous inventors and their inventions?

Take suggestions. If any of the following are mentioned you may want to elaborate, or you may want to select a few others from the list.

Thomas Edison invented the phonograph – later called the gramophone – which was the first kind of record player.

Dr Edwin Land invented the Polaroid instant camera in 1944. He had noticed how a child was disappointed because when she had her photo taken she couldn't see the result straightaway.

Ladislao and Georg Biro invented the ball point pen in the 1930s.

Georges de Mestral invented Velcro after noticing how grass seeds stuck to his socks when he was out walking.

Inventions

George Otis invented a safety device that would stop a lift from falling if the cable broke.

In 1901 King Camp Gillette invented the safety razor with throw-away blades. Before them, all men had shaved with a long open razor blade – more like a knife blade really.

In the 1960s Mary Townsend invented the extension lead with three or four sockets in it that means you can plug a number of things in to one socket in the wall.

William Painter invented the crown bottle top (the kind you lever off with a bottle opener).

The list is endless because people are inventing things all the time.

Has anybody here ever had a bright idea for a new invention?

Take some ideas and be encouraging. Children often have lateral thinking brainwaves which are amusing or give food for thought.

All of you would really please a man called Trevor Baylis, who lives in a house by the water on Eel Pie Island on the River Thames.

Trevor has had an interesting life. He didn't do too well at school but later he went to evening classes to do engineering.

In the 1950s he swam backstroke for England.

Later on, he used that swimming ability, working as a swimming pool salesman and giving demonstrations of underwater and trick swimming.

Once he was on television, swimming with a killer whale at Flamingo Park in Yorkshire. Eventually, Trevor had his own swimming pool company.

Trevor had always been an inventor – constantly thinking up solutions to problems,

and making things in the workshop behind his house.

In the 1980s he invented a can opener that you could use with one hand. Who might need a can opener like that do you think?

Take suggestions.

Well, it would be used by someone with a disability or weakness that prevents them from using two hands to handle a can and an opener.

Trevor's single-handed can opener was a big success, and he went on to invent lots of other useful things for people with disabilities.

But recently he had an idea for a new invention, and it's turned out to be a very big idea indeed.

This is the story of his big idea.

📖 Story

One day, Trevor was watching the television.

It was a programme about the spread of HIV infection in Africa.

The illness HIV is a very serious problem in parts of Africa. The programme explained that the difficulty is how to tell people about the danger and about how to prevent the spread of infection.

The presenter of the programme said that a good way of telling people, especially in remote villages, was through special programmes on the radio.

The trouble was, though, that lots of these villages have no electricity. This means that people run their radios on batteries.

Now you know how annoying it is when batteries run out. For us it's easy to buy new batteries. But in an African village it's a different matter.

To the people in the villages batteries are very expensive. They are also difficult to buy – they often have to travel a long way to find them.

Because of this, people only listen to their radios for a short time each day.

This means that they don't usually want to spend their precious radio time listening to programmes about HIV either. They want music and entertainment.

Trevor watched all this and thought about how much better it would be if the people could listen to their radios all the time, without worrying about batteries.

He remembered that when he was young, instead of CD players, people had gramophones on which to play records.

You had to wind up the gramophone – with a handle. It had no battery and no electricity.

It worked from a spring motor – a clockwork motor.

You wound the spring up tight and then as the spring slowly released, it drove the gramophone turntable.

So, wondered Trevor, why not have a wind-up radio?

He set to in his workshop and built the first clockwork radio. He made a small, spring-driven motor that drove a small electric generator.

The generator made enough electricity to make the radio work.

Of course, there were all sorts of little practical problems to solve, like what sort of spring to use, what sort of wires, and so on.

But he did solve all the problems and now there is a factory in South Africa that makes what they have called Baylis radios – named after Trevor.

A Baylis radio looks exactly like any other sort of small radio except that it has no batteries or mains lead.

It just has a little turning handle that you wind it up with.

It takes one minute to wind it up, and it will then play for an hour before you need to wind it again.

Trevor was very pleased with his invention. He knew that it would make a big difference to the quality of life and also to health education in lots of places in the world.

Now, people all over Africa, and in other parts of the developing world where there is no mains electricity and where batteries are scarce, will be able to listen to the radio all day.

They can listen to music whenever they like and have the time to listen to other programmes, too – news and information programmes.

All they have to do is twiddle the little handle occasionally to keep the generator going.

Inventions

✦ Conclusion

I think that people in this country might like to buy a Baylis radio, too.

What do you think?

There must have been lots of people watching that same television programme as Trevor, who all thought how good it would be if the African people could have a different kind of radio. But unlike Trevor, most of them would not have thought that they could do anything about it, and would soon have forgotten about it.

Trevor spends a lot of his time trying to encourage young people just like you to have bright ideas.

His message to you is that when you have bright ideas you shouldn't forget about them. See if you can do something about them instead. Who knows, you may turn out to be a famous inventor.

And even if you don't become famous, you may be able to help to solve a problem for somebody who needs help.

☀ A prayer

Dear God, we thank you for all the people who have invented things to make our lives easier. We thank you especially for those like Trevor Baylis who are helping disabled people and people in the developing world, where resources are scarce and where it's hard to make a living. Amen.

☀ A thought

Will you have a bright idea today?

Everyone has bright ideas. You don't need to be good at any particular subject. You just have to think of a problem and a way of solving it. You can use those ideas to make others' lives easier and to cheer people up.

Song suggestions

'The building song', *Come and Praise*, 61

'This little light of mine', *Alleluya*, 14

Optional follow up

- Ask children to think about an invention or inventions which they think would be useful.

- Ask children to draw and annotate an illustration of such an invention.

- Contact a local group for the disabled or elderly and invite someone into school to show a range of specially designed equipment.

- Identify three inventions in the classroom and try to spend a day without using them. You might try the door handle, a board wiper and scissors, for example.

Juggling

This is an assembly about juggling – the art of doing several things at the same time. It draws a parallel between actual juggling with balls and a mum who juggles her life so as to keep everything going.

You will need

- a blank OHT and a pen

- a book for the volunteers to read from.

Taken by	....	....	....
Date	....	....	....
Given to	....	....	....

Comments

- ....
- ....
- ....

✦ Introduction

As this assembly is about juggling, check whether any child can actually do it. It would be a pity to miss the opportunity.

Who can do more than one thing at once?

Let's see.

Try rubbing your tummy and patting your head at the same time.

All do it. Say 'Change hands,' a couple of times.

Now, let's see who can read a book out loud and write their name on the OHT at the same time.

Choose some volunteers to try this. It's not at all easy, especially for a young child. Let adults join in. If any find it easy, make the test harder, eg. to write the name of the school and the school address.

I think there are people in your house who have to do more than one thing at the same time – look after a baby, cook the dinner, listen for the doorbell to pay the milkman.

Can you think of anybody who has to do those things?

Take suggestions.

I call it juggling when someone has to do lots of jobs and fit them all in. But juggling is also doing tricks with juggling balls. Like the boy in this story.

📖 Story

Mr Swanson's class had got around to discussing what they were going to do when they left school.

'I'm going to be a doctor,' said Nina. 'I'm going to get lots of A levels and go to university. Then I'm going to be a doctor and cure people of all sorts of diseases.'

'I'm going to work in an office,' said Sal, 'and go to work in a BMW and wear smart clothes.'

'I'm going to be a vet,' said Ashok. 'I'll work with animals all day long and make them better when they don't feel well.'

Juggling

Mr Swanson turned to Philip.

'Well, Philip,' he said. 'What are you going to do?'

'I'm going to be a juggler,' said Philip in a very matter of fact way. 'I'm going to work in a circus and I'm going to juggle.'

Everybody burst out laughing at that, including Mr Swanson.

Philip felt quite upset and he kept quiet after that, because he didn't want to be laughed at.

But what the class didn't know was that he was a juggler already – not a very expert one, but at least he could do it.

This is how it happened.

One day, Philip was visiting his grandad, when his grandad asked, 'Would you like an orange, Philip?'

Philip said he would and he walked over to the fruit bowl and picked out an orange.

While he was looking in the bowl, his grandad said, 'Throw an orange over to me, Philip.'

Philip picked out an orange and tossed it over to his grandad.

He was quite surprised though, when his grandad threw it up in the air and caught it in his other hand. Then he stood up, still throwing the orange up and catching it, and he called to Philip, 'Come on, Philip. Throw me another!'

Fairly timidly, Philip threw another orange over. His grandad caught it with one hand and started throwing that up and down too, at the same time as the other one.

Then he said, 'Right, another one, eh?'

So Philip threw another orange and, lo and behold, his grandad was juggling three oranges – throwing them up so that they went in a steady stream one after the other, up and over into the other hand and across back to where they started.

It looked really spectacular.

Philip's grandad laughed and started to talk in little bursts, without taking his eyes off the flying oranges.

'I … didn't know … I could still … do this, Philip!' he said.

'I used to be … quite good … WHOOPS!' (He nearly dropped one and had to reach out to grab it before it hit the sideboard.)

He kept going for quite a while and then started to do some different things.

He threw one orange up from behind his back so it came over his shoulder.

Then he turned his hands over and started catching them with his hand facing downward – sort of snatching them in the air.

Eventually, he dropped one. He made a desperate lunge for it, but it got away from him and bounced on the hearth.

He caught the other two and flopped down in his chair.

'That was good,' laughed his grandad. 'I used to be really good at that. I thought I'd forgotten how to do it.'

Philip was fascinated.

'Can you teach me?' he asked.

His grandad nodded and replied, 'It's practise mainly. Tell you what, I'll see if I can find my

Juggling

old juggling balls, and we'll have a go next time you come.'

So the next time Philip went down to his grandad's flat, his grandad had found his juggling balls.

They were just the right size – smaller than tennis balls but larger than golf balls. They were soft, not bouncy, and covered with lovely coloured leather.

'Right,' said his grandad. 'First just hold one in your hand and then take another in the same hand and throw it up and catch it in the other hand. Then throw it back again, still holding the first one.

'Concentrate on throwing very carefully, just the right height, so that you don't have to reach too far for it.'

That was the start. Philip concentrated hard and practised every day. His grandad kept giving him tips.

After just one week, he could juggle three balls very easily. In fact, he could soon take over from his grandad – his grandad would juggle the balls and Philip would just walk over to him and take the three balls without stopping them.

Philip's mum was amazed by it all.

'I remember Dad used to juggle for us when we were little,' she said to Philip. 'But I haven't seen him do it for ages. And now you're doing it. Who would have believed it?'

So when Philip told his teacher that he wanted to be a juggler, it really wasn't as far-fetched as it sounded.

Philip told his mum that night and she said, 'Tomorrow, when I take you to school, I'll bring the juggling balls and you can show Mr Swanson.'

The next day, Philip's mum didn't leave him on the playground, she took him into school.

They found Mr Swanson in his classroom, with Miss Pike, the headteacher.

'Hello,' said Philip's mum. 'I thought you might like to see Philip juggle.'

She got the juggling balls out of her bag and passed them to Philip.

'Off you go, Philip,' she said and Philip did his stuff.

The two teachers were really surprised and they clapped when he finished.

'Brilliant!' said Miss Pike. 'Mind you, I know where he gets it from,' she added.

Philip and his mum were both surprised, and Philip's mum asked, 'How did you know his grandad taught him to juggle?'

Miss Pike laughed, 'I didn't! I meant from you!'

'But I can't juggle!' said Philip's mum.

'Oh, I think you can,' said Miss Pike. 'I think anybody who manages a family like you do is a very good juggler.'

Philip's mum shrugged her shoulders, but Miss Pike carried on.

'You have three children – one here, one in the infants and one in a pushchair. Each week day, you take two of them to school and one to nursery. Then you go off to work in the

Juggling

hospital. Then you come and pick all three of them up – one after the other. Then you take them home, sort them out and give them their teas.

'You never miss a parents' evening and you're on the PTA committee. Sometimes you even come and help in class when you have an afternoon off. That's just like keeping a lot of juggling balls in the air all at the same time. Just as clever I reckon, and a lot more tiring. I think all mums are good jugglers. What do you reckon, Philip?'

Philip understood very well what Miss Pike was saying. He knew his mum sometimes flopped down feeling very tired, but she always had time for a laugh and she was always interested in what he was doing.

'I get it from both of you – Grandad and you, Mum,' he said.

'Good answer!' said Mr Swanson. 'Very diplomatic.'

✦ Conclusion

Why do you think Philip, his grandad and his mum were all jugglers?

Philip and his grandad could juggle with juggling balls – throwing them up and catching them, three at a time.

His mum couldn't do that, but she could keep a lot of things going at the same time – looking after the family, doing a job, giving love and affection.

Lots of people are like that. They can't sit around for long, because there's too much to do and not enough time to do it in.

If your family has jugglers in it – people who work hard and then come home to do lots of jobs – try to appreciate them and say thank you from time to time.

☀ A prayer

Dear God, thank you for two kinds of jugglers. Thank you for the ones who can do tricks, make us laugh and keep us entertained. And thank you for the ones who do lots of jobs and keep us safe, well fed and looked after. Amen.

☀ A thought

Do you appreciate the jugglers in your house? Try to say thank you to them and try not to give them too many extra jobs to do.

Song suggestions

'Supermum', *Tinder Box*, 24

'Hands to work and feet to run', *Someone's Singing Lord*, 21

Optional follow up

- Talk about other circus images that are used to reflect real life – 'balancing act', 'being on a high wire', 'acting like a clown'.

- Ask the children to think of phrases used in sport that might provide images for real life.

Gran the typist

Assembly 3 of 4

In this assembly, a child discovers that his gran has a hidden talent, and he realises that writing on a computer may be an older skill than he previously thought.

You will need

- the OHT provided

- a computer keyboard, pens and pencils.

Taken by ....

Date ....

Given to ....

Comments

- ....

- ....

- ....

✦ Introduction

In this assembly we are going to look at writing. In school we do a lot of writing using pens, pencils and computers. It's an important skill, that helps us make our way through life. Being able to write in a particular way can change a person's life – and I'm not just talking about being a famous author.

Hold up, in turn, a pen, a pencil and the keyboard.

What do all these have in common? Of course, they are all used for writing.

Which one is the easiest to use?

Take suggestions.

All the answers are right, in a way. It all depends on how expert you are and what sort of work you want to do.

If you wanted to do a beautifully lettered certificate, you'd use a pen.

If you wanted speed, then you'd go for a keyboard.

If you wanted to make some quick notes in a lesson or on a school visit, you might use a pencil and a notebook.

The computer keyboard is quick if you know how to use it. Some people can touch type. This means that they use all ten fingers and hardly ever look at the keyboard.

Put up the OHT provided.

You start to learn the 'home keys' – placing the four fingers of your left hand on A, S, D and F and three on your right hand on J, K and L.

Either of your two thumbs uses the space bar.

Your little finger on your right hand can then stretch to the right where all the punctuation keys are.

Now put your fingers on your knees and we'll do some touch typing.

Point to any of the 'home keys' and let the pupils follow by typing on their knees.

That's about as far as we can go without having a keyboard each, but you can see the idea.

Gran the typist

You start with the home keys, and then learn to move your fingers up and down to the keys on the other rows.

Your fingers learn the right positions so that you hardly have to think about them, and you can concentrate on what's on the screen. When you first see good touch typing it looks like a sort of magic.

That's the experience that Robert had.

📖 Story

'What's that?' asked Robert's gran.

Robert had come in from school and produced an interesting looking green object from his school bag.

It was a curvy shape, with a built-in handle.

'Is it a handbag?' she asked innocently.

Robert snorted. 'Not a handbag. It's an E-Mate.'

'A what did you say? An E? And don't call me mate. I'm your old gran. Show some respect.'

'No,' sighed Robert. 'It's called an E-Mate, and it's a little computer. We've got some in school and every so often we can bring one home if we have some work to do on it.'

'Let's see it then!' exclaimed Robert's gran.

Robert put the little computer on the kitchen table, and opened the lid. The screen was on the inside of the lid.

It was already on, because the computer switched on automatically when the lid was open, and the last piece of work was displayed on the screen.

Robert's gran peered at the screen.

'A bit dim' she said.

'I don't think you are,' said Robert. 'I think you're quite clever really.' Then he laughed.

'Cheeky beggar,' said his gran. 'Now brighten that writing up if you can.'

Robert pressed a little button at the top of the rows of keys and the screen lit up so it was easier to read.'

'Much better,' said his gran. Then she was quiet for a moment as she read what Robert had written on the screen.

'Did you do this?' she asked.

'I did,' said Robert. 'All by myself.'

'It's very good really,' said his gran. 'A story about a lost sheep. From the Bible is it?'

Robert nodded.

'We did it in RE,' he said. 'We have to write a modern version of it. But I decided to start by writing out the story from the Bible, just to remind me.'

'Take you long?' asked his gran.

'Ages,' said Robert. 'Copying it from the Bible. And I've only just started.'

'Fetch my Bible from my room,' said Robert's gran. 'I'll finish it for you.'

'But you can't...' said Robert.

'Can't what?' said Robert's gran. 'Can't use the computer? Maybe not. But I can see it's got an ordinary keyboard. You just set it up and I'll do the rest.'

So Robert went and collected his gran's Bible from her bedside table.

He leafed through the soft thin pages of the Bible until he found St Luke's gospel, chapter fifteen.

Gran the typist

'Now set up the computer for me,' said Gran as she sat herself down in front of it.

Robert opened up a new document. 'It's ready now. You just type,' he said.

'Read out the story to me,' said Gran. 'My eyes are a bit old for dodging to and fro to that small print.'

So Robert began, at verse four.

'What man' he said slowly, and then stopped. He looked at his gran. She looked back at him. 'What are you waiting for?' she asked.

'For you to type what I said,' said Robert.

'Don't be daft, lad,' said his gran. 'Just read. I'll do the rest.'

So Robert started again, and this time he kept going.

'Suppose one of you has a hundred sheep and loses one of them – what does he do?'

He stopped again, just in time to see his gran's fingers flying over the keys and her eyes fixed on the screen.

She stopped.

Robert swallowed and went on.

'He leaves the other 99 sheep in the pasture and goes looking for the one that got lost until he finds it. When he finds it, he is so happy that he puts it on his shoulders and carries it back home. Then he calls his friends and neighbours together and says to them, "I am so happy I found my lost sheep. Let us celebrate!" In the same way, I tell you there will be more joy in heaven over one sinner who repents than over 99 respectable people who do not need to repent.'

Robert stopped again and in about five seconds his gran had caught up. She stopped.

'There. All done. How long did that take? Two minutes?'

Robert just stared at her. He went and looked at the screen. 'There might be a couple of mistakes,' his gran said. 'I'm a bit out of practice, and this keyboard is a bit small and light. But I haven't lost my touch.'

Robert was speechless.

He had known his gran all his life, and had never suspected that she had this great skill.

'How did you learn to use a computer? You've never had one,' said Robert.

His gran laughed. 'No. But I did have a typewriter,' she replied. 'And twenty-five years of secretarial work. So I can touch type – and that works just as well on a computer. Better in fact, because the keys are light and you can really fly along.'

'Touch type?' asked Robert.

'I use all my fingers and my thumbs, and I don't look at them. I just look at the paper – the screen now I suppose – and keep an eye on what's coming out. I don't need even to think about my fingers. You should learn. It will make all the difference to the way you use that little thing. It certainly changed my life.'

'How?' asked Robert.

She turned to face him and Robert sat down on the other kitchen chair.

She began. 'When I was fourteen, I left school. My two brothers and my dad were coal miners. My older sister, Sarah, had gone off to be a housemaid in a big house in the town. I tried a few shop jobs, including one picking up clothes from customers for a laundry. I hated it.'

Gran the typist

She paused as she remembered it.

Then she carried on, 'My mum knew that I could do better. So she sent me to a private teacher to learn shorthand and typing. I still don't know how she afforded it. My dad was very tight with his money, and she must have gone short of all kinds of things for herself so I could learn. I passed my exams in shorthand and typing, and when I was fifteen I got a good job in the tax office. It was like a different world.'

'How do you mean?' asked Robert.

'Well, my home was a rough sort of place. Can you imagine, three miners coming home to a small house, all dirty because there were no baths at the pit then. Then at the tax office there were quiet folk in suits and dresses, and it was as if I had started a new life, which I had really. I was so grateful to my mother. And I still am. Without her I would never have had a good start in life. I would never have met your granddad, never have had my lovely family.'

She smiled at Robert and said, 'My mother knew me, just as the shepherd knew every one of his sheep. So my new skills went on to change my life. My mother was determined I wasn't going to get lost you see.' 'Maybe that can be the story I write for my homework,' said Robert.

'Why not?' said his gran. 'Better start now. You might be finished in time for the Millenium!'

And she mimed picking at the keyboard with one finger, her tongue sticking out of the corner of her mouth. They both laughed.

✦ Conclusion

Robert's gran was rescued in a way, like the lost sheep.

The Bible story tells us that the shepherd left his flock to go and look for the lost sheep. I suppose Robert's gran's mum did the same in a way.

She didn't leave the rest of her family, but she quietly concentrated on the one who needed her for a while.

I think all of us do that sometimes. It might happen in your own family – one person needs more attention for a while, and it's something we have to understand.

☀ A prayer

Dear God, we thank you that we are well looked after, like the lost sheep. Help us to recognise when some people need more help than we do for a while. Let us give support to those who need it. Amen.

☀ A thought

Finding the things we are good at is not always easy. When we find them it can change our lives.

Song suggestions

'I did it!', *Primary Assembly Song Book*, 87

'One more step', *Come and Praise*, 47

© **pfp** 2002 ISBN 1 874050 56 2 May be photocopied for use only within the purchasing institution **pfp**, 61 Gray's Inn Road, London WC1X 8TH

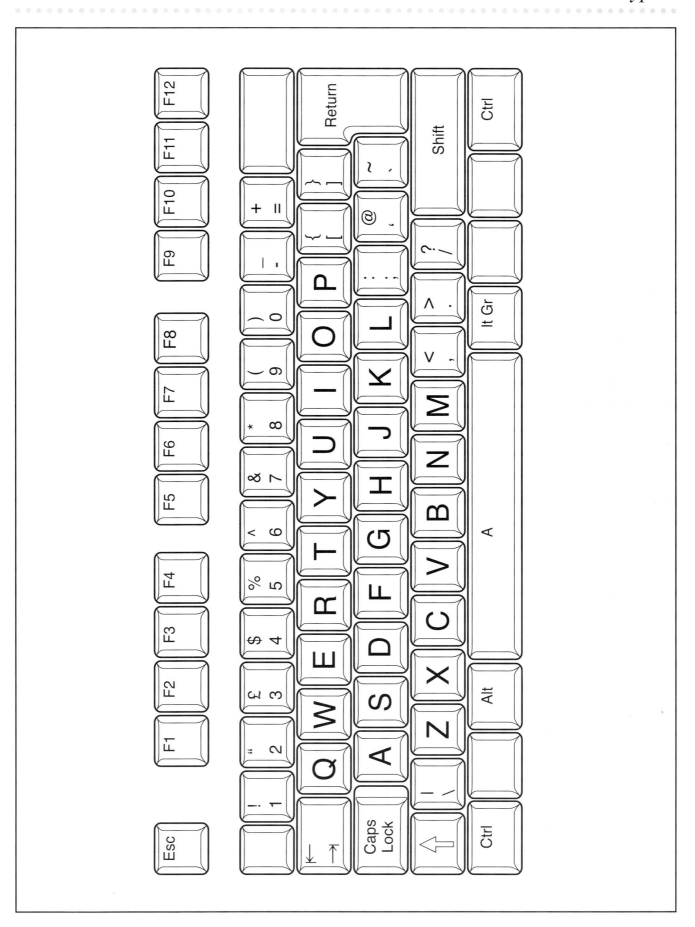

Gran the typist • OHT

The race is not to the swift

Assembly 4 of 4

This assembly is about a child who discovers that she has a talent of her own, different from the netball ability that she once admired so much. The message is that, although we need role models, we need to think how we choose them, and not simply follow the crowd.

You will need

- nothing at all.

Taken by ....

Date ....

Given to ....

Comments

⬤ ....

⬤ ....

⬤ ....

✦ Introduction

Why do we race and run marathons? To prove to ourselves that we can do it. But what if the thing we want to do is not what we are really cut out for? It may be time to look for something else, the story today shows us.

Do you look up to somebody? Is there somebody you would really like to be? Or somebody you want to be like? That's not a bad thing. We all learn from watching others, and we all gain inspiration from being with people who are good at what we want to do.

We have to be careful, though, not to be led along the wrong path. We can strive to be like somebody even though we are never really going to be able to do it. Sometimes, that can lead to unhappiness. There's a time when you have to stop and think whether you are doing the right thing.

Here's an elderly lady talking about when she was at school.

📖 Story

Long, long ago, when I was a little girl, we used to go out onto the playground for our games lessons. We had no field, just an asphalt yard, with some markings on it. We did, though, have some netball posts, and netball was one of the favourite games. It wasn't my favourite, though.

The teacher used to leave us very much to our own devices at games time. When it was our turn for netball, she would gather us together and then she would bring two girls out to the front and tell them to pick two teams for netball.

Looking back, it always seemed to be the same people who were fetched out to the front. Perhaps there were others, but I don't remember them. The teacher would say, 'Margaret! Jane! Pick your teams and get the game started.' Then she would go off to see to some other children at the other end of the playground.

Margaret and Jane would usually decide who had the first pick. Sometimes they did 'paper–scissors–stone', sometimes they just

The race is not to the swift

remembered who had first pick the last time. Then, while we stood there they would take it in turns to pick from among us.

I hated it. I really, really hated it. Why? Because I was always the last to be picked. Not the next to the last. Always the very last. The good players would go first, and when there were two or three on each side they would start whispering into Jane's or Margaret's ear. 'Pick Stephanie next,' or 'Get Becky now.'

But nobody ever said, 'Quick! Pick Polly.' There were about three of us who were always left at the end. The really humiliating thing was that neither Margaret nor Jane nor any of their best players wanted to pick us at all. They'd rather have played without us, even if they didn't have as many players. They would look at the three of us, and time would go by, and eventually Margaret or Jane would say, 'Oh, come on then Mary,' and 'OK. I'll have Sue.' And I was always left standing there. They would actually all turn and start moving to where they were going to play and I would still be standing there, and sometimes I'd have to say, 'Whose team am I in?' and Margaret would probably say, 'You have her, Jane.'

Did I say I hated it? Well, I'll say it again. I really did hate it more than I can say.

The worst part is I really wanted to be good at netball. The problem was that the girls I looked up to were good at sport. Even though girls like Margaret and Jane treated me as if I was nobody at all, I still looked up to them and wanted to be like them. It seems pathetic now, but that's how it was for me. I would follow them around and be on the edge of the groups of their friends. I wasn't the only one who did that, but I was more on the edge than any of the others.

I really tried to get better at netball. I'd bounce up and down on my feet, trying to look alert and capable like the other girls. Then I would try really hard to catch the ball cleanly and pass it sensibly to someone. But it never seemed to go right. As often as not I would fumble the ball and drop it on the ground. Or I would hesitate and my pass would be intercepted. Or I would pass it to entirely the wrong person – sometimes I'd even get so flustered that I'd pass it to a member of the other team. Everyone would get on at me then, and call me names. 'Polly, you're useless!' they'd say. And they weren't joking either. Their faces would show that they really meant it. It hurt me very much, and the more I tried the worse it got.

Eventually, I became really unhappy at school. My mother wondered what was the matter with me. The funny thing was I never tried to get out of games lessons. I suppose it was because I always thought, each time, that this was the day I would suddenly be very good. I would give a dazzling performance and everyone would admire me, and I would never be the one left out ever again. But of course it was never like that at all.

I would have been unhappy all through school, and perhaps beyond school, if something hadn't happened that changed my life.

We had a new teacher. She was different from the other teachers somehow – she smiled a lot for one thing, like your teachers do now I suppose. Practically the first thing she did was to decide to put on a play for Christmas. She wrote it herself. It was a sort of pantomime really, based on 'Aladdin and His Wonderful Lamp'. I wasn't going to ask to be in it, because I just assumed I'd be no good. But she sought me out – I still don't really know why, unless she saw something in me that others hadn't seen. She told me she wanted me to play the part of Aladdin. Me! I thought I wouldn't be able to do it, but I did. I learned

The race is not to the swift

my lines, and I learned lots of actions, and do you know I found I could make people laugh, or even cry. The audience loved me, and I suddenly became famous in the school.

It wasn't just that, though. What being in the pantomime did was to make me realise that being good at netball wasn't the only thing worth doing. In fact, after being on the stage and taking a bow with lots of people cheering, being good at netball seemed a small thing.

The funny thing is, that that teacher moved on quite quickly, and I didn't do much acting after she'd gone. But I realised that I enjoyed learning my lines, and understanding the words, and that I could be really good at English. I started to write poems and stories, and soon everyone in school knew me for that. In my final year, I won a national poetry prize and I was in the paper. I became a star pupil, like Margaret and Jane – and I think I was a better person for the way I got there.

Writing things – poetry and stories – has given me pleasure ever since. I've never been famous for it, but I know I can do it. I still like to watch netball – it's a good game. I might even have been better at it if someone had helped me a bit more. But it doesn't matter now. I found something I was good at. I suppose that's part of growing up – trying to find your own thing, that you are good at, and not just trying to follow everyone else.

✦ Conclusion

The Bible tells us that, 'The race is not to the swift nor the battle to the strong.' (Ecclesiastes 9:11) I think that means that the road to success is not always the obvious one. You look down life's road, and you think you can see the best and quickest way. But perhaps there are other ways which are less obvious.

You may find another way for yourself, or you may need a little help. Our best hope is that we, your teachers, will help you to find your own best way. Or it may be your family or your friends who eventually guide you on the path that is best for you. In the meantime, don't always be too quick to follow, or try to prove that you can do something that, in your heart, you know is not for you.

☀ A prayer

Lord, help me to find the way that suits me best. Help me to see that when I long for strength and speed and quickness of mind and eye, I may find them in different ways and different activities from those of others. Amen.

☀ A thought

'The race is not to the swift nor the battle to the strong.' Think what this means in your own life.

Song suggestions

'My Little Island', *Primary Assembly Song Book*, 88

'Light up the Fire', *Come and Praise*, 55

Optional follow up

- Ask the children in pairs to write down the other person's strengths and then exchange the lists. Any surprises? (Tip: Don't do weaknesses.)

What is bullying?

Assembly 1 of 4

This assembly concentrates on the issue of a child who is drawn unwillingly into bullying her own friend.

You will need

- the OHT provided and a piece of paper to cover it.

Taken by ....

Date ....

Given to ....

Comments

● ....

● ....

✦ Introduction

What is a bully?

Look at the OHT and tell me which of these sentences fits someone who is a bully.

Put up the OHT provided. Reveal the first sentence.

A bully is someone who hits other people.

Put your hand up if you think that a bully is someone who hits other people.

Reveal the next sentence.

A bully is someone who threatens other people.

Put your hand up if you think that a bully is someone who threatens other people.

Reveal the next sentence.

A bully is someone who makes fun of other people.

Put your hand up if you think that a bully is someone who makes fun of other people.

Reveal the final sentence.

A bully is someone who is afraid to stand up for what is right.

Put your hand up if you think that a bully is someone who is afraid to stand up for what is right.

The last definition is likely to cause some confusion and is dealt with later.

Now let's just run through those.

A bully is someone who hits other people, yes. Some bullying is physical – a person is hit or jostled in queues or pushed.

Let me give you an example.

Jamie is being bullied by Tom. Every time Jamie gets near to Tom, Tom kicks him on the legs and ankles. Jamie has bruises on his legs and ankles. His mum notices them, but Jamie is afraid to tell her what the problem is and makes up stories to explain them.

Jamie is being made unhappy by this and he is certainly being bullied.

But not all bullying is physical, is it? Some children are very unhappy about being bullied, and yet they haven't been hit or pushed at all.

Often a bully is someone who threatens. You know the kind of thing – someone says, 'I'm going to get you after school,' or 'If you don't

What is bullying?

give me your sweet money, I'm going to beat you up.'

That's certainly bullying, even if they don't actually carry out the threat.

Let me give you an example.

Bella is afraid to go home from school, because Clare and her friends have threatened to wait for her and get her. So every day Bella hurries to get out of school first. Being so afraid, she sometimes tries to go a long way round, which is very dangerous because of the traffic and because her mum doesn't know where she is.

Bella is being made unhappy by this and she is certainly being bullied.

What about making fun? Well, that can be part of bullying, can't it? It can be name-calling or cruel jokes.

Let me give you an example.

Khalil has prominent teeth at the front. His mum likes them and has always thought they were attractive. But Khalil is very self-conscious about them. A group of people in the class make it worse by calling him nasty names and imitating his teeth.

Khalil is being made unhappy by this and he is certainly being bullied.

Now there's the last one we saw on the OHT.

A bully is someone who is afraid to stand up for what is right.

That's a bit confusing, isn't it? But it's true of a lot of people who end up being labelled as bullies.

Let me give you a longer example to explain this one.

📖 Story

Lisa was one of a group of very close friends. There was Jane, Laura, Chloe and Michelle. There were some others too, but those five were really the main group.

They sat near each other in class, whenever the teacher would let them – sometimes he split them up on purpose. They always went around together at playtime, dinnertime and after school.

Michelle was very much the leader of this group. She had a strong personality and was fond of telling the others what to do.

Lisa had some other friends of course. One of them was Natalie, a very quiet girl who was good at most of her work.

Natalie sometimes went around with the others, but a lot of the time she preferred to be on her own. In class, she liked to just get on with what she was supposed to be doing.

Lisa liked Natalie a lot. Lisa's mum liked her too and was always wanting Lisa to bring Natalie round to the house.

One day, Lisa was talking to Natalie at playtime. Michelle and the others were some distance away and they kept looking across at Lisa and Natalie.

When Lisa had finished talking to Natalie, she walked over to join the others.

Michelle looked at her and said, 'We've decided we don't want Natalie with us any more.'

Lisa was surprised. 'Why not?' she asked.

'She's a snob,' answered Michelle. 'And we don't like her. So stop talking to her if you want to be our friend.'

This was a shock to Lisa. 'She's not a snob!' she said. 'Why is she a snob?'

© **pfp** 2002 ISBN 1 874050 56 2 May be photocopied for use only within the purchasing institution **pfp**, 61 Gray's Inn Road, London WC1X 8TH

What is bullying?

Michelle said, 'She just is.'

In the days that followed, Lisa felt very torn. She liked Natalie a lot, but it was very important to her to be part of Michelle's group.

In the meantime, Michelle and the rest of the group became more and more cruel towards Natalie. They would snigger behind her back, hide her sports bag and call her names.

Lisa tried to keep out of it, but she was so desperate to keep in with Michelle and the others, that she too began to stare at Natalie and pull faces along with the others.

Lisa's mum was puzzled.

'Why doesn't Natalie come round any more?' she asked. 'You were such good friends. What's gone wrong?'

Lisa would look away and make an excuse. 'She's been off ill for a bit,' or 'She's been busy with her violin lessons.'

Then came the day when the whole thing got a lot worse. Michelle told Lisa and the others that they were going to get Natalie after school.

All day Michelle threatened Natalie under her breath. Natalie looked white and really unhappy.

After school, Natalie tried to run off before the others came out, but they caught up with her in the cul-de-sac around the corner from school.

Michelle snatched Natalie's bag and threw it over a hedge. Lisa stood there feeling really bad, but she didn't do anything.

When the others started chanting terrible things about Natalie, she joined in.

Natalie looked at her with tears in her eyes, and that made Lisa feel even worse.

The chanting stopped as a car pulled up alongside them.

Out stepped Mr Townley, their teacher. He saw straightaway what was happening.

After he had put Natalie in his car to take her home, he wrote down everyone's name.

Lisa was mortified, because she knew there was big trouble coming.

The next morning, nothing happened for a bit, and everyone was very quiet in class.

Towards dinnertime, people in the class started to be sent for one by one by Mrs Mercer, the headteacher.

The day wore on. Natalie went down to the headteacher's room and was there a long time.

Then other people were sent for. Some of them didn't come back.

Out of the window, Lisa was shocked to see Michelle going home with her mum.

Then the secretary came in.

'Can we see Lisa, please?' she asked.

Lisa went into Mrs Mercer's room. She wished the floor would open up, because there was her mum, with a white face and tears starting in her eyes.

'I've had to tell your mum,' said Mrs Mercer. 'I've told her that you appear to be a member of a group of girls who have been bullying Natalie Weston. Now I thought you and Natalie were friends, and when I spoke to your mum she wanted to be here so that we could ask you about it together.'

Lisa muttered something and looked at the carpet.

'Speak up, Lisa!' said her mum sharply.

What is bullying?

Lisa said, a little louder, 'It was Michelle. She made me do it.'

Lisa's mum made a really loud angry sound.

'She made you do it?' she cried. 'She made you bully your good friend? How could she do that? Couldn't you tell her where to get off?'

Lisa was in turmoil inside and was really upset because her mum was so angry.

'I can't understand it!' her mum said. 'How could you be cruel to your friend?'

Mrs Mercer shook her head.

She knew how difficult it was to deal with this sort of thing. She knew how much influence one person in a group could have on the others.

All the same, she was really disappointed that Lisa hadn't been able to stand up for what was right.

'I didn't have you marked down as a bully, Lisa,' she said.

This shocked Lisa even more as she thought, 'Me a bully? I'm not a bully! Am I?'

✦ Conclusion

Well, was Lisa a bully?

A bully is anyone who behaves in a bullying way. A bully is an ordinary person who for some reason does cruel things, either occasionally or more often.

It doesn't matter if they start the bullying or if they just go along with it. They still make the person they are bullying feel unhappy and afraid.

If someone lets bullying happen and doesn't stand up against it, they are really just joining in.

Bullies need to think of others – of how the person who is being bullied feels. And they need to think about themselves – why they are deliberately hurting someone. They won't do that unless somebody speaks up about it.

If Lisa had stood up to Michelle and said, 'No, I'm not doing this,' some of the others might have stood by her. Perhaps they just needed a little push to do the right thing.

Then Michelle would have been on her own, and she would have been made to think about what she was doing.

☀ A prayer

Dear Lord, help us to always have the courage to stand up for what is right even when it seems very difficult. Help us to always care for other people and not deliberately hurt them. Amen.

☀ A thought

Standing by and just letting bullying happen is just like joining in with it. Let us all try to stand up for what is right, no matter how difficult it may seem.

Optional follow up

- Draw up a classroom code of conduct.

- Link bullying to 'stalking' issues. Stalking is bullying without actual physical harm.

- ## A bully is someone who hits other people.

- ## A bully is someone who threatens other people.

- ## A bully is someone who makes fun of other people.

- ## A bully is someone who is afraid to stand up for what is right.

Hope

Assembly 2 of 4

What does hope mean? What makes someone hopeful or hopeless? This assembly looks at a homeless person and considers how attitudes to people can affect the way they see the world.

You will need

- nothing at all.

Taken by ....

Date ....

Given to ....

Comments

⬤ ....

⬤ ....

✦ Introduction

For each of the following questions encourage the children to join in with the response 'I hope so'.

Will it be a nice day today?

I hope so.

Will we win the match?

I hope so.

Will Jane be in when we get there?

I hope so.

Will we find our way out of here?

I hope so.

Will my verrucca get better?

I hope so.

We use the word hope when something bad or something good might happen, but we would rather think of the good thing happening.

We do like to hope for the best thing. It's a lot better than fearing that something will go wrong.

Suppose we answered the same questions in a much more gloomy way.

Will it be a nice day today?

No. It will be terrible.

Will we win the match?

Not a chance.

Will Jane be in when we get there?

You're joking. She's always out.

Will we find our way out of here?

No. We will be in here for ever, walking around in circles.

Will my verrucca get better?

No. It will grow huge and horrible until you can't get your shoe on and everyone will point at you and pull a face.

We really can't carry on like that, can we? We have to hope and look forward to something better.

I was joking then, but there are many more serious examples.

When someone is out of work, they have to hope that they will get a job. When someone is

Hope

ill, they hope that they will get better.

In fact, if you hope for good things, it can help them to happen.

A sick person who is hoping to get better sometimes feels a bit stronger and more able to fight the illness.

A person out of work who hopes for better things will look more cheerful and might be more attractive to an employer.

The opposite of hopeful is hopeless. That's a terribly sad word.

A person who has lost hope is hopeless and has nothing to look forward to.

There are people in the world like that. Think of someone who has lost their family and home in a war or a famine. Think of someone who has no job, no home and no prospect of either.

Here's a person who is almost hopeless, but manages to keep going. This is Jim's story.

📖 **Story**

Hi. I'm Jim. I live on the streets of the city with Rex, my dog, because I have no other home.

I'm afraid I wasn't very well behaved at home and my parents weren't very patient with me, so I left when I was sixteen. I didn't get on with my dad and I don't keep in touch.

I hitchhiked to London because I thought I would get a job there.

When you see London on the TV, you see people living in nice flats, walking around with briefcases and working in good jobs.

I just thought I would be able to do all that.

I was a fool. What was I going to do in a T-shirt and jeans, scruffy and straight off a truck that had given me a lift?

Let me tell you how daft I was.

I went into a big office block and asked if there was a chance of a job. The girl on reception just looked at me. She picked up the phone and a man came out.

Looking back, I suppose I was lucky. He could have been really sarcastic and nasty – lots of people are like that to us you know.

Instead, he was rather kind really. He just said they had all the people they needed, advised me to get some qualifications, wished me luck and sent me on my way.

I did get bits of work. I found if you went to the back door of a big hotel you could sometimes get work scrubbing pans or cleaning the kitchen.

It's dreadful work though and there's hardly any money in it. Sometimes, you get some decent food, but not very often.

One chap stopped and offered to help me once.

He bought me a coffee and talked to me, but I was suspicious of him. I thought he was trying to make friends for reasons of his own, so I walked away from him.

He swore and shouted after me. That made me sure I'd done the right thing.

Anyway, I've just plodded on like that for a year now.

If I manage to get a bit of money from work or from begging, I might sleep in a hostel.

If I haven't any money, I sleep on the street.

Hope

Sometimes I sleep on the street anyway and save my money for food or a drink.

I have a couple of places where I sleep. There's a quiet shop doorway in a side street. That's usually OK and I have a blanket round me.

Sometimes, drunks kick me in the night – or do worse things – but not very often.

The police leave me alone because they know I won't do any harm.

Another place is under the railway bridge.

A lot of us sleep there. But it can be dangerous, because there are people who are unstable. They can be violent.

Still, it's out of the rain and usually there's a fire to sit round.

What do I hope for? I still hope that I'll get that job and a nice flat. But I don't know how I might do it.

Look at me. Would you give me a job if I walked into your office? My hair's a mess. I can't shave properly. My clothes are rubbish.

The longer I'm like this, the less likely I am to get a job.

As it is, I haven't really any training. There was so much trouble at home that I hardly went to school and I don't read and write all that well.

With no job, I won't get anywhere to live.

With nowhere to live, it's difficult to get a job, because I have no address for anyone to write down.

So I'm sort of trapped in a way. Funny isn't it really?

I have to hope though. I can't give up.

There are people on these streets who have given up. They are just getting through each day. The old ones are waiting to die I think. There's nothing else for them.

The worst thing is thinking that you are nobody.

People walk past and look at me as if I'm muck.

Sometimes people mutter at me – scrounger and things like that. But I'm a person, aren't I? If I'm not a proper person, then what am I?

If you took any of those well-dressed people who look down on me, took their clothes off them and dressed them like me, they'd be just the same, wouldn't they?

I hope something will happen. Somebody will give me a chance and train me to do some proper work. It will happen. I'll get a job and a flat.

Meanwhile, there's old Rex here. I got him from someone who couldn't look after him anymore.

Rex likes me and he's always pleased to see me. Nobody else is pleased to see me.

Rex would miss me if I wasn't here. Nobody else at all in the whole world would miss me if I wasn't around.

That's a frightening thought isn't it? But I have to keep hoping, don't I?

✦ Conclusion

Hopelessness is a terrible thing. Jim is nearly hopeless, but he's clinging on.

What doesn't help is that other people won't give him any hope. People look down on him and treat him like he's not a proper person.

© **pfp** 2002 ISBN 1 874050 56 2 May be photocopied for use only within the purchasing institution **pfp**, 61 Gray's Inn Road, London WC1X 8TH

Hope

If a few people stopped to talk to him, encouraged him and gave him some confidence, he might do better.

No one should look down on Jim. He is a person like the rest of us – loved by God as all people are.

Let me tell you what Jesus felt about this.

He said one day to the people around him, 'Do you know something? I was hungry and you did not feed me. I was thirsty and you gave me no drink. I had no clothes and you did not give me any. I was in prison and ill and you did not visit me.'

The people around him were surprised. They cried out, 'We haven't done that! How could we do that! Tell us when we did these things. Tell us when you were hungry and we did not feed you. Tell us when you were thirsty and we gave you no drink. Tell us when you had no clothes and we did not give you any. Tell us when you were ill in prison and we neglected you.'

Jesus said that God's reply was, 'If you have done any of these things to any person, then you have done them to me.'

Jesus meant that it's no good believing in goodness and kindness unless you actually do the good and kind actions yourself. If you don't, you are letting your beliefs down.

Other world religions would agree with that, because it is about the way we treat each other.

That's a good lesson. It tells us that all people are loved by God and their lives are valued by him.

It is our duty to remember that. We should keep alive people's hopes by treating them properly and giving them attention when they need it.

At school, we do it by having charity collections and events. But we also need to keep other people's hopes alive by respecting them and by treating them as we want to be treated ourselves.

☀ A prayer

Dear God, we ask you to keep hope alive in people for whom everything seems hopeless. Remind us that everyone is of equal value in your sight. May we show that in our school by encouraging and respecting each other. Amen.

☀ A thought

Could Jim do more for himself? Some people might think so. But that shouldn't change the way people treat him. If people treated him well, he would feel better about himself and might then see ways of improving. In any case, true love and concern is unconditional – it is freely given, with no thought of how it is received.

Song suggestions

'How we treat each other', *Primary Assembly Song Book*, 66

'Streets of London', *Alleluya*, 41

Optional follow up

To introduce the issue of homelessness, read *Street Child* by Berlie Doherty (Collins 0006740200) for the true story of the orphan who inspired *Dr Barnardo and Monkey Island* by Paula Fox (Orchard 185213852X) for a story about a family living rough in New York.

Refugees

Assembly 3 of 4

This assembly is about what it is like to be seeking refuge in the UK at the end of the twentieth century. It reminds us that children are always the innocent victims, and that all religions remind us of our special duty of care towards them.

You will need

- nothing at all.

Taken by	....
Date	....
Given to	....

Comments

- ....
- ....

✦ Introduction

Today's assembly is about a child and his family from a different part of the world who have had to overcome difficulties to try and build a better life for themselves. We will hear about some kind people who helped them to do that.

Do you know what a refugee is?

The word 'refuge' means 'a safe place'. So a refugee is someone who is looking for a safe place.

It's usually someone who has had to leave their home or their town or their country because of fighting or other kinds of danger. Then they go somewhere else – perhaps to another country – in search of a safe place.

Sadly, we have seen too many refugees on television in recent years – people driven from their homes, usually by war. The saddest victims are children. They are innocent victims. Whoever is to blame, it cannot be them, and yet they suffer the most.

Listen to Suli, a refugee, who tells us of her feelings.

📖 Story

I am Suli. I live with my mother and my father. We all live in a room together, but it does not feel like a home to me.

We did have a home once. It was a nice house, in a village where we had many friends. I went to school there, and I did well at my lessons.

Then one night everything changed for us.

There were gunshots in the street, and a loud banging on the door. The door burst open from the outside, and masked men came in, carrying guns.

They made my father give them our money, and our identity cards and our passports.

They beat my father with their guns. Then they suddenly turned and went away.

We helped my father to stand. 'We cannot stay,' he said. 'The next group that comes will kill us, or will separate us from each other.'

So, in the dead of night, we left our house and our village, and all our friends, and the life that we knew, and got into a minibus with blacked-out windows.

Refugees

It took us to a house in another country – I do not know where it was – and we were hidden there in an attic.

Then we were put into the back of a big lorry, in a tiny space among the cargo that the lorry was carrying. In that lorry we escaped to England.

Now, we live in a small town in England. We do not know if we can stay here, but we know that we cannot go back.

We have no house of our own. My father and mother are not allowed to work to earn money. We live in one room.

My mother cries a great deal. My father tries to cheer us up, and speaks always of better times to come. He has great faith that we will do well in this country.

'When I can work, we will find a nice house, and everything will be fine, you'll see!' he says, but as he turns away his eyes tell a different story.

There is something, though, that really upsets me. The people who looked after us when we arrived, and found us this place to live, are kind. But the other day I was shouted at in the street by a group of young men and boys. Their faces were angry, and they were pointing and chanting.

It frightened me because it reminded me of the terrible night when the men in masks came into our house.

And then the other night, a brick came through the window of our room. We heard shouts and jeers, and saw young men running away. My mother became hysterical.

'We have come all this way and it is starting again!' she said.

My father tried to console her, but you could tell that he too was upset by what had happened. He shook his head and said, 'What do they think we can do to harm them?'

There is one bright spot, though. I have started to go to school. It is strange in many ways – the language is difficult, and the ways of working are not what I am used to. But what warms my heart is that in my school there is real kindness.

My teacher knows I am sad, and she puts her arm round me. She has told the other children to be understanding to me, and they come to me and offer sweets and friendship.

Everyone is kind. The ladies who give us our dinner make a fuss of me, and sometimes try to give me extra food, but I do not want to be different. I want to be one of these children, a part of all that happens.

So tomorrow I will see if I can join the choir. I was in the choir at my school back home, so perhaps this is something I can do to link together my old home and my new one. I hope so.

Perhaps it can be a new beginning for me. And I know that if I can be happy, then my father and my mother will be a little more happy too.

Refugees

✦ Conclusion

There have been refugees since the beginning of history. Jesus was born away from his mother's home in a stable. Perhaps there will always be refugees.

Jesus, like all the main religious leaders, tells us that we must have room in our hearts for all people in difficulty. Above all we must remember that children, always, are innocent victims. Sometimes the people have come for the sake of their children, to find a better life for them. If we can make the children welcome, then we will be going a long way towards making all the refugees welcome.

☀ A prayer

Oh Lord, you were homeless as a little baby. Be with all refugees. Give them comfort and safety, and help us to accept them with love into our own communities. Amen.

☀ A thought

If a person is a refugee, it is because of something that somebody else has done to them. People do not usually choose to leave their homes and arrive penniless in another country.

Song suggestions

'One more step', *Come and Praise*, 47

'How we treat each other', *Primary Assembly Song Book*, 66

Optional follow up

Look at the great refugee movements through the twentieth century – track them on a map. Try to find out what makes a person leave everything to come to another country.

We shouldn't laugh

Assembly 4 of 4

Children sometimes make fun of disabled or mentally ill people or others who seem 'different'. Developing a proper, more emotionally mature response is part of growing up. This assembly is intended to help children to learn that.

You will need

- nothing at all.

Taken by ....

Date ....

Given to ....

Comments

● ....

● ....

● ....

✦ Introduction

In today's assembly we are going to look at feelings that bring on laughter and think about when that laughter is appropriate and when it is not.

We all like to laugh, but sometimes we need to think carefully about whether we are laughing at the right time.

One of the things that we have to learn as we grow up is that laughing at people who can't defend themselves, or who don't even know they are being laughed at, is always wrong, no matter how tempting it might be.

If the people who laugh only stopped to think carefully about what they were doing, they probably wouldn't do it.

📖 Story

'Look!' said Phil. 'Here comes Raymond!'

Phil was on his way home from Linford Primary with his group of friends. The others turned and looked up the road, smiles already forming on their faces.

Along the road came a strange figure on an old bike. He was dressed in a heavy black overcoat, and a black trilby hat. His trousers were baggy and black, held in by bike clips, and on his feet he was wearing big black boots up to the ankle.

Phil and the others – Jack, Sam, Dev and Lucy – lined up along the pavement.

'Hello, Raymond!' shouted Phil. 'Stop! Stop! Your back wheel's going round!'

Raymond stopped and put a foot down and looked at the little group of boys and girls who were standing there with big grins on their faces. He turned round to look at his back wheel.

We shouldn't laugh

'Have I got a puncture?' he asked.

'Oh no!' said Sam, laughing. 'Your tyre's just down a bit, but only at the bottom!'

The others all sniggered. Raymond got off his bike and held it while he had a look at his back wheel and tyre.

'What's the matter with my bike?' he asked, with a worried look on his face.

'It's got you on it!' shouted Dev, in a loud voice. Then he looked at the others and they all nearly had hysterics.

Raymond now realised that they were making fun of him. He stood up and looked at them.

'Don't laugh at me,' he said. 'It's not right. You shouldn't laugh at me.'

'Well,' said Lucy, 'what else are we supposed to do? You're just too funny, Raymond. So we just have to laugh at you.' Then she shouted, 'Daft Raymond! Daft Raymond!' and ran off down the street. The others ran after her, looking back over their shoulders and shouting, 'Daft Raymond! Daft Raymond!'

Raymond stood looking after them. He said, 'You shouldn't laugh at me. My mum said…' But they couldn't hear him. In the end he got back on his bike and slowly pedalled off.

. . . .

So far as the children were concerned, that seemed to be the end of it. They'd had a good laugh. They talked about it for a few moments, and then they carried on.

But Raymond didn't forget it so easily. 'I have to try to remember not to come down here when the children are coming home from school,' he thought to himself. 'But it's difficult to know the right time. I wish they wouldn't laugh at me.'

That might have been the end of it, except for Mrs Jackson.

Mrs Jackson had just come out of the butcher's when she heard the commotion on the other side of the road. She heard and saw everything that happened.

The next day, she went into Linford Primary and asked to see Mrs Stanwick, the headteacher. Luckily, someone else was taking assembly so Mrs Stanwick had some time to spare. Mrs Jackson went into Mrs Stanwick's office. The door closed behind her, and she was in there for quite a long time.

Eventually Mrs Stanwick showed Mrs Jackson out and took her to the door. She had a very serious expression on her face and she was shaking her head.

'I'm really glad you told me, Mrs Jackson,' she said. 'And I'm sorry that children from this school have been so cruel. I shall deal with it this very morning.'

When she had seen Mrs Jackson out, she w ent into the secretary's office and said, 'After assembly, I want to see Phil Morgan, Dev Rooprai, Sam Bond, Lucy Maxwell and Jack Vincetti in my office. Straightaway.'

The five friends stood in a line in front of Mrs Stanwick's desk. She didn't waste any time.

'Last night,' she said, 'you were seen making fun of Raymond Timpson in the High Street on your way home from school. What have you got to say?'

They were all quiet, all thinking different things. One of the things they were all thinking, though, was that Raymond had another name. Raymond Timpson. They had never heard that before. Raymond Timpson. It made him sound like – well, a proper person.

'Well?' said Mrs Stanwick. 'I am waiting. Phil? Why don't you start?'

Phil couldn't quite see what the big problem was. 'It was only fun, Miss,' he said. 'We were just having a bit of fun with Raymond. You see he's, well…'

Dev broke in, 'He's not all there, Miss.' He said it as if he was carefully explaining something that Mrs Stanwick didn't know.

Mrs Stanwick's face didn't change, but her eyes glinted a bit. Lucy noticed it. But the others didn't.

Then, abruptly, Mrs Stanwick shoved her chair back and stood up. The others flinched at the suddenness of it.

'Come with me,' she said. The five children walked after her as she strode off down the corridor. She turned into the library, then she turned to them. 'Sit down,' she said.

They sat down on some of the chairs that were pulled into a circle ready for somebody's circle time. Mrs Stanwick sat on one of the others.

'Now listen,' she said. 'I'm going to tell you a story. It's about a boy called Raymond Timpson.'

The others looked at each other. This was not quite what they had expected. They sat there looking at Mrs Stanwick.

• • • • • • • • • • •

'Raymond was born thirty-eight years ago. He was quite ill when he was first born, and nobody expected him to live. He lay, a tiny scrap of a baby, in an incubator. His mum sat and watched, and prayed for him to stay alive.

He did live, and he grew strong in his body. But he was slow to learn to talk and walk, and when he started school he found everything difficult. He couldn't make friends easily either. He was unhappy at school because he was bullied. The other children taunted him and called him daft Raymond. In fact some people have called him daft Raymond all his life. He must have heard it thousands of times. And it hurts him every time.

He had no real friends. His best friend was his mum. If she heard people calling him names she would come out of the house and chase them away. He thought the world of his mum.

Then, six years ago, his mum died. Ever since then he's been completely on his own. Social Services keep an eye on him and the Methodist minister pops in. But that's it. No friends, no job, and just the memory of his mum, the only friend he had. That's Raymond Timpson, the man you clever lot made fun of in the street. Think about it. That's all. Off you go.'

The five friends didn't say a word. They just filed out of the library. They had some thinking and some talking to do.

After school, they were lined up again on the pavement when Raymond came along. 'Oh no,' thought Raymond. 'I've done it again. The kids are coming out of school. And here's that lot again.'

Once again, it was Phil who shouted to Raymond to stop. But he said it in a different sort of voice. 'Please stop, Raymond,' he said. 'We just want to talk.'

Raymond, always eager to please, stopped by the group of friends, but there was still some anxiety in his face. 'What's up now?' he asked.

'We just want to talk,' said Lucy. 'Where've you been?'

We shouldn't laugh

'I've been down to the church,' said Raymond. 'To where Mum's grave is. I go every day.'

He was very suspicious. But the children chatted to him for a bit and then said goodbye.

Perhaps twice a week after that, Phil and his friends stopped to chat to Raymond. Gradually he grew to trust them, and soon he began to enjoy their company, and they enjoyed his. He knew a lot about the town, because he spent his days cycling around it.

It was during one of their meetings that Mrs Jackson came out of the butcher's. She looked, and there was Raymond, stopped by the roadside. And there were those five children, and – she could hardly believe this – they were laughing again.

She frowned, and was making her mind up to go across, when she saw there was one crucial difference between the scene now and the scene that had made her so angry a couple of weeks before. When she looked more closely, she could see that the faces of the children were different. The cruelty had gone, and the laughter was somehow warmer and easier on the ear. And, most important of all, this time, Raymond was laughing too. Instead of the five children laughing at Raymond, all six were laughing together.

And the interesting thing was that the five friends felt a lot more comfortable with that sort of laughter than they did with the laughter that came from being unkind.

✦ Conclusion

Do you ever laugh at anyone like Raymond? At any man, or woman, or child whose behaviour is a bit different?

Perhaps that's not a fair question, so I'm going to ask you a different one.

When I read out the story did you laugh? Did you think Raymond was funny when I described him? Do you think any of the things the children said to him were funny? I think some of you did, because I heard you. Now I'm not blaming you for that, because it was just a story. But I think it shows how easy it is to fall into the trap of laughing at someone.

There's plenty of laughter in the world, plenty of good things to enjoy, lots of good jokes. So there's no real need to laugh at anyone who isn't enjoying the experience and can't laugh with you.

☀ A prayer

Lord, we thank you for what the prayer book calls 'all sorts and conditions of men' – for the fact that we are all different from each other, men and women, boys and girls. Help us to resist the temptation to laugh at the differences you have created in us. Amen.

☀ A thought

If you can't laugh with someone, then don't laugh at them.

Song suggestions

'The family of man,' *Come and Praise* 69

'Make me a channel of your peace,' *Alleluia* 43

Optional follow up

Laughter can be cruel. Think of times when you have laughed and you shouldn't have. Make a list.

Little 'un

Assembly 1 of 4

This is an assembly for at or near the end of the summer term, when people are facing change and uncertainty. It looks, indirectly, at how the most valuable protection for the times ahead is self-confidence and self-knowledge.

You will need

- nothing at all.

Taken by ....

Date ....

Given to ....

Comments

⦿ ....

⦿ ....

⦿ ....

✦ Introduction

Another school year is coming to an end. As it's gone on, we have all come to know one another. Each class has been together for nearly forty working weeks. In that time, people have made friends, and formed groups.

For many of us it all feels comfortable. We've become used to our surroundings and the people we are with. We don't want to leave it all.

Most of us are going to have a change, though. We may be going to a new class, or even a new school – and that applies to teachers as much as to pupils. Some teachers are leaving, and many will be teaching different classes. So we all feel uncertain.

As we leave the school year behind, and go into something more uncertain, I wonder what is the most valuable thing we can take with us? Let's hear the story of Melanie.

📖 Story

It was July, and Melanie was close to her last week at junior school. She wasn't really looking forward to the secondary school. She had been on visits, and the teachers there had been to see her class more than once, but it all seemed a bit big and forbidding somehow. Not as comfortable as the juniors. After all, she had not always been happy even at her small junior school.

It wasn't that she was bullied. On the contrary, people seemed to like her well enough. She was, though, a bit fed up with herself. She didn't always like the way she looked, and she thought that the way she looked might lead to trouble in the secondary school.

So what was Melanie worried about? Well, if you had to write a list of words to describe Melanie you might put 'pretty', you would probably say 'happy' and you could include 'noisy' – all these are possible.

But the one word that is certain to be on everyone's list is 'small'. Or 'tiny'. Or 'little'.

Little 'un

For Melanie is what the fashion writers call 'petite', which those of you who've done a bit of French will know is simply French for 'small'. And by that I don't mean 'young'. She was ten years old and half the seven-year-olds at school were taller than her. If they gave her a chair that fitted her, her chin didn't come up to the tabletop. If they gave her a chair that was right for the table, then her feet swung four inches above the floor.

So, all you average-sized people, can you imagine what life's like for those who aren't? Well, they sort of stand out, don't they? They get called names. Melanie was addressed as 'Titch', 'Tiny', 'Midget', among others that hurt, and even the affectionate names, like Dad calling her 'Little 'un', made her just a bit sad. Also, when you're small you are less strong, and more easily pushed around.

• • • • • • • • • • •

The adults in Melanie's life – her relations, her teachers – tried to ease things for her by saying, 'It's quality that counts, not quantity,' or 'Little and good, that's the way to be.' But Melanie said, 'If smallness really is unimportant, there wouldn't be all these sayings about it, would there? After all, people don't make up excuses about having blue eyes, or being left-handed.'

Once in assembly the children were told an old tale about a man who had three sacks, and the biggest one boasted of its great size and importance (it was one of those stories where sacks could talk). The second sack, although not quite as large, was also very pleased with itself. The third was hardly a sack at all, more of a bag, and far too insignificant even to speak. Anyway, when the man reached the market the first sack was opened to reveal

potatoes and it was put in the open. The second contained flour so it was stored under cover. But the smallest was taken with great care to the jewellers, for it held precious diamonds.

Well, stories like that were well meant, but were obviously just intended as a comfort. 'The only people who need comforting,' Melanie thought to herself, 'are those who've got something wrong with them.' So, far from making her feel better such stories in fact made her feel worse – they simply made her think that she was odd, a freak!

Her dictionary piled the agony on even more, for there she discovered that 'small beer' is a weak drink suitable for children, that a 'smallholding' is a piece of land not big enough to be a real farm, that 'small-talk' is trivial, unimportant chatter; that 'to feel small' is to feel humiliated, that 'to sing small' is to use a humble tone of voice or to apologise. Everything, it seemed, about the subject of size assumed that bigger meant better. So obviously smaller must mean worse.

• • • • • • • • • • •

Most of the time Melanie didn't let all these sad thoughts show. She kept up a brave front. Indeed, on occasions she fought back with flying fists and shrieking voice and she sorted out people twice her size. But she couldn't think quickly enough to reply to the jokes of friends like Uncle Trevor who said that 'every family needed one person small enough to be shoved in through the lavatory window if the front door key got lost'. She wasn't very happy either when her class was doing the Victorians, and the teacher told her that she'd have made a fortune in those times sweeping narrow chimneys.

Little 'un

On the whole, though, Melanie felt she could handle things in the juniors. But what would it be like in the secondary school, with everyone towering over her, and yet more jokes and nicknames?

One day, after a bad dose of teasing, she was walking though the park, her eyes filled with tears that were half of self-pity, half of anger, when a voice said, 'You'll make it rain, young lady.'

She looked out from her wet hanky and was very surprised to see her grandad sitting on a bench under the big chestnut tree. Grandad was always ready to listen and was the only person in her family who had never teased her about her size. Her sadness just poured out and Grandad listened without interrupting until her words dried up. Then...

'You see my big nose,' he said. 'It's no use being all polite. I know that you all think I've got a big nose. Red, into the bargain. A big, red nose... Well, when I was a kid they called me 'Jumbo', yes, and 'Hooter' and – what else was it? – ah! that's it, 'Conk'. Some of them who still live round here still use my old nicknames.

'There aren't many of them left, of course, because I've seen most of them off now. But let's see, there's 'Flapper' Davis. He wears his hair long now to hide those ears of his, but when we were lads we all had short back and sides and they stuck out like sails on a ship. And 'Pig' Sewell. My golly he could eat, he could, and noisy with it – never shut his mouth, you could see his dinner going round like a cement mixer.

'Then there was my best mate 'Pongo' Taylor, so called because of his not washing often

enough. Oh yes, young lady, you can laugh...' (for by this time Melanie's tears had disappeared) '...but those names we gave each other took a bit of getting used to.'

Grandad paused and sat looking into the distance. Melanie thought that perhaps he was looking back into the past, too, remembering things he'd done and friends he'd known years before.

'I've learned a few things through living so long,' he said after a while, 'and a couple of them might be useful to you in the state you are in now. The first thing is that when you're young you want to be like everyone else. You hate it when you stick out of the crowd. You want to dress like your friends dress, ride the same bikes as your friends ride. You don't want in any way to be out of the ordinary.

'I thought them making rude comments about my nose was nasty and cruel because I wanted my nose to be like everyone else's – but I thought my mentioning their peculiarities (Flapper's ears, Pongo's smell), well, that was just a bit of fun. What I didn't know until we were grown up was that they too had suffered. So, you're not alone, my love, and that makes things better, doesn't it?'

Melanie nodded. It was always better not to be the only one.

'The second thing I learned,' Grandad went on, 'is that as you get older the things that make people interesting are not their similarities but their differences. Not the ways in which they are the same but the ways in which they are unique. Oh yes, I'm quite proud of my old nose now. It's one of the things that make me me, if you see what I mean.'

He whistled and a dog appeared from behind the bushes. 'Home!' Grandad said. 'That's a Jack Russell. She's the sixth I've had. I'd not

Little 'un

have a different breed than a Jack Russell. Let others have Alsatians, Old English Sheepdogs and the like. Give me a small dog anytime. Mopsy here is just the right size for me. I feel comfortable with her. Wouldn't want one a penny bigger.'

As she watched her grandad tread heavily off – Mopsy at his side, her little legs going ten to the dozen – Melanie thought of those to whom she too was 'just the right size', those who didn't tease her. And she realised there were far more of them than those who did. So, when Jane (with the freckles) came up to her and said 'Hello, Squirt', Melanie didn't reply 'Hello, Spotty' as she usually did but simply said, 'I'm going on the swings. Coming?'

✦ Conclusion

Melanie didn't get any taller after she had talked to her grandad. The rest of her family and her friends didn't stop mentioning her smallness, or calling her names. She still got upset sometimes. But the talk did make her think. She started to realise that we really are all different from each other, and that it's our differences that make us interesting.

When she went to secondary school, she didn't find it easy. Some of the other children towered over her. But she found that as she grew older, more and more people just accepted her for what she was, and liked her very much. Her form teacher was very good. He never once mentioned her smallness and he made a point of taking her very seriously. In a way, he was carrying on where Grandad left off. Some of the other teachers did the same, and gradually she became more and more confident and happy.

The most important thing we can do in the future is to have confidence about ourselves and help others to have confidence by not making unnecessary fun of them.

☀ A prayer

Dear God, there are things in this life that hurt me. People often cause me a lot of pain, not because they are deliberately cruel but because they don't think.

And I do the same to other people. Help me to put myself in their place and try to understand how what I do and say affects them.

And if they do the same we shall all stop hurting each other. The best way for me to cope is for me to know that I am myself and that just as God takes me as I am, so will other people if I show them the same respect. Amen.

☀ A thought

A dozen times a day I seem to come up against this problem – that what I want to do for myself will hurt or inconvenience other people. There is so often a clash between myself and the concern I should have for others. First, I must know myself and respect myself. Then I must show the same respect for others.

Song suggestions

'Moving on song', *Alleluya*, 39

'Give me oil in my lamp', *Come and Praise*, 43

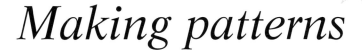

Making patterns

Assembly 2 of 4

This assembly is about a special carpet with a pattern in it that symbolises the weaver's life. It shows how a pattern can have a deep meaning.

You will need

• the OHT provided.

Taken by ....

Date ....

Given to ....

Comments

⬤ ....

⬤ ....

⬤ ....

✦ Introduction

This assembly is about a special person who makes a very special pattern that tells the story of his whole life.

📖 Story

It was hot in the little house that special day. Through the open window came the voices of children playing outside, and the sunlight streamed in and shone on the back of Fanji the weaver as he sat at his wooden loom.

His hands were busy choosing coloured threads and knotting them into the warp and weft of the carpet that he was making.

He had no paper pattern and no instructions. His mind's eye saw the pattern that he wanted to make, and his fingers obeyed his instructions.

His had been a hard life, with some sharp corners – his father had died when he was small, and his mother had had to work very hard to keep the family together. Often there

had been very little food in the house. But what he remembered was the sound of his mother singing. She always sang, no matter how sad and worried she was. In fact, she seemed to sing more when she was feeling down, and it lifted her spirits and reassured her son of her love.

Of her love there was no doubt – at times of great difficulty, Fanji always took comfort from her promise that they would always stay together.

The years went by and Fanji grew strong enough to work. At first he helped his mother in the fields, working beside her in the heat of the sun and in the drenching rain of the wet season, always hearing her voice as she sang and chanted to encourage the seeds to germinate and the crops to grow.

Grow, my seeds, be tall.

Search upwards for sunlight and rain.

Grow, my seeds, be strong.

Search downwards for richness of soil.

Grow, my seeds, and ripen.

Making patterns

Grow, my seeds and feed my children.

Grow, grow, my seeds.

At the loom, his hands stopped as the song came back to him. The sun on his back through the window was the sun that beat on his back in the fields all those years ago, and the voices of the children outside were the voices of his childhood friends.

He stopped work for a while, and let his mind wander to those far-off days.

He remembered the time when he became old enough to learn the trade of the weaver, and he sat for hours under the watchful eye of one of his uncles as he learned to handle the thread, and to make the knots that gave the carpet its pile and its pattern.

At first he was slow, but as the months went by his fingers and hands grew stronger. He began to put his own ideas into the patterns – subtle variations, changing colours and new shapes.

His teacher marvelled and, in time, Fanji became one of the best carpet weavers the country had ever known. His mother never again had to work bent double in the sun and rain in the fields.

Yet Fanji never stopped being a simple weaver. He never married, and when his mother died, he continued to live in her small house.

'Why would I want a big house?' he would say. 'I need only one bed to sleep in, one room for my loom and one table at which to eat my food. This is enough for me.'

The day that the sun shone into Fanji's house and his mind filled with memories was a special day, because it was the day that Fanji would finish his last carpet.

'I am old,' he said to those who visited him that morning. 'My eyes are tired and my hands are stiff. I must stop now. I do not want to make carpets that are not as good as my best. So this is my last one, and it has my life within it.'

At the end of that special day, Fanji's last carpet emerged from the loom. Fanji took it out into the sunlight and laid it gently on the ground.

Put up the OHT provided.

It made a splendid sight and his friends gathered round to look. They looked at the patterns and one of the women said, 'Tell us the meaning of your carpet, Fanji!'

Fanji stood by his carpet and pointed to it and told the story.

'There are two halves, showing the early part of my life and the later part. In the early part, at the bottom of the carpet here, is a pattern that represents the shoots of growing plants, reminding me of when I was a child, new in the world and growing strong. They remind me, too, of the work I did in the fields in those far off days.

'Here is the burning sun and the rain that fell as we worked. The dark jagged shapes are for the difficulties and bad times that we had when my father died. All around here is a vine, a sign of my mother's love entwined around us.'

The crowd looked closely and Fanji continued.

'Here in the centre is a symbolic tree – myself, stronger now and confident, standing alone, but with roots fixed firmly in my early life, and branches extending upward into better times.

Making patterns

'Here is the later part of my life. The jagged shapes have gone. The feeling is gentle and mellow. There are torches of flame – burning lights that represent my desire to create my carpets. There are many many flowers. Each of these small flowers is one of my customers. The larger flowers, though, stand for you, my many friends, bringing colour and beauty into my life.'

The woman asked, 'What is this at the top?'

Fanji answered, 'It is the beginning of a road. We cannot see where it goes, but it invites me to step out and follow it where it leads. My weaving days are finished. A new road beckons me. All around the border of my carpet is this strong pattern that symbolises God's protection, with me all the days of my life, pulling in all of its parts together and giving them meaning.'

✦ Conclusion

Many patterns have meaning – a simple checkerboard pattern can say things about light and darkness, day and night. A pattern of interlocking circles might stand for the way that all of us are linked together in our lives.

Choose the right patterns, as the weaver did, and you can tell quite a complicated story.

Perhaps you can make a carpet pattern that tells your own story?

☀ A prayer

Dear God, we thank you for the patterns in our own lives – the rhythm of day and night, the interlocking circles of our friendships. Help us to understand the patterns and to make sure that they have the right kind of meanings. Amen.

☀ A thought

Our minds are made to see patterns. When we have seen the easy ones, it is time to look harder for the hidden ones.

Song suggestions

'Make me a channel of your peace', *Alleluya*, 43

'A wonderful thing', *Primary Assembly Song Book*, 32

Optional follow up

Devise carpet patterns that tell stories – about children's lives, ambitions or favourite events. Encourage symbolism rather than straight representation.

Making patterns

Making patterns • OHT

Speaking up about bullying

Assembly 3 of 4

Speaking up can be difficult. This assembly is about a boy with learning difficulties who is bullied by a group of other children. In the end one of the other boys plucks up the courage to speak up and things begin to get better.

You will need

- a whistle (optional).

Taken by	....	....	....
Date	....	....	....
Given to	....	....	....

Comments

● ....

● ....

● ....

✦ Introduction

Blow the whistle if you have one.

This week, I read about a man who was called a whistleblower. He hadn't really blown a whistle, but what he had done was spot something going wrong in the place where he worked, and he had done something about it – I suppose a bit like a referee spots something wrong and then blows his whistle.

He had found out that some of the people who worked at the same place where he worked were stealing money from the firm.

Now it took a lot of courage for the man to speak up. He felt very much alone, because quite a lot of people were involved in the stealing, including some who were much higher up than him. At first, nobody wanted to listen to him – they told him to go away and forget about it – but he kept on until he found people who would listen, and eventually the thieves were arrested and sent to prison.

It takes courage to speak up when you see something wrong going on. That's because there are things that stop you. Here are some of them.

You might end up falling out with your friends.

The people in charge might think you are in the wrong, and you will get into trouble yourself.

The people doing the wrong things might threaten you or do you harm.

You just don't like telling tales.

The man I told you about could have thought all of those things, but luckily he didn't. He knew what he had to do, and he spoke up.

Here's the story of another whistleblower. He had the kind of problem that might affect any of you.

📖 Story

Tim was being bullied at school. He didn't realise it at first. Tim was a good-natured boy who thought the best of everyone. He used to talk to a group of lads at break and lunchtime. They stood around and chatted and fooled

Speaking up about bullying

about. Tim thought of them as his friends.

Gradually, though, the lads that Tim talked to at break started to be nasty to him. They would make fun of him, and Tim would join in the laughter, because he didn't realise that the lads were laughing at him.

They would send Tim off on errands to fetch them things – 'Go and get my ball, Tim, hurry up!' one of them would say, and the others would say, 'Yes, Tim, hurry up. Go on! Go on!' And Tim would still laugh, because he thought he was helping the lads and being a friend to them.

Gradually it got worse. The lads started asking Tim for money. Tim was a kind boy and he would get his money out and give it to what he thought were his friends. They said they would give it back to him, but they never did. So Tim didn't have money for lunch or for sweets at break time.

Then when Tim was running off to fetch them things, the lads would throw stones at his legs. 'See Tim! That'll make you run!' they would say.

• • • • • • • • • • • •

Tim had no way of coping with this at all. He was a gentle lad, with learning difficulties, and he had only ever been treated kindly before. He was a popular boy in his family, and he simply could not understand that anyone would want to be unkind to him.

He didn't want to leave the group of lads, because he thought of them as his friends. One of the things he did at home was an impression of Elvis Presley. Everyone liked it when he did that, so he thought if he did it for the lads at school they would like him more. But when he tried it they laughed and jeered.

After that they would make him do it again and again, and Tim didn't really know whether they liked it or not, but he felt there was something wrong with their reaction.

Tim grew very quiet at home. When his dad asked him about his friends, he would grow angry and say, 'I have got some good friends, Dad, I have!' and his dad would shake his head and stop pestering him.

It got worse and worse – Tim was being pushed around and made to do all sorts of things. The lads were very clever, though, and if anyone came up to them, or if one of the playground supervisors looked at them, they would pretend to be playing.

• • • • • • • • • • • •

There were five lads in the group. There were Andy, Geoff, Simon and William who joined in everything and there was Rob, who was the leader. Rob was the one who egged everyone on. The others joined in because they wanted to do what Rob did.

All except William.

William grew more and more uneasy about what they were all doing to Tim. He knew it wasn't right. But he also felt he had to do what Rob did. He didn't want to fall out with Rob and the other lads. He hadn't any other friends, and it was a good gang of lads to be in.

One night he couldn't sleep. He kept thinking of Tim running off to do errands, turning round and laughing, and he and the others pretending to laugh but really jeering and making fun. 'I can't stand this any longer,' he thought to himself.

Speaking up about bullying

Next morning, Jim, William's mum's fiancé, was getting him his breakfast, because his mum had gone off to work early. He liked Jim a lot, and he decided to tell him what was going on.

'Jim,' he said. 'I'm a bully!'

Jim laughed at first. He thought it was a joke. 'Yeah, Will, so am I. Come here and I'll duff you up!'

But William didn't laugh. He shook his head. 'I really am. I've been making fun of one of the kids with special needs, and being cruel to him.'

Jim sat down across the table and looked at William. 'Tell me more, Will,' he said. And William told him the full story. It sounded awful when he said it all out loud, and William horrified himself by putting it all into words.

Jim was quiet for a bit, then he said, 'It's a case of following the crowd is it not, Will old lad? Haven't I told you that you do too much of that? Is it that Rob? Is it?'

William looked down at his cup and just nodded. Jim made an angry sound. 'Hah! How often has your mum told you about him? He's got no sense him. What are you playing at? You've got more brains than him in your… well, I won't say it.'

'What shall I do, Jim?' asked William.

'Simple!' said Jim. 'And you know already. You go to the headteacher and you tell him what's going on. As soon as you get to school. Do you realise how much harm you lot have been doing? Tchhhh!' and he made that angry noise again.

'I daren't, Jim!' said William. 'Rob'll come and get me, and I won't be friends with his lot any more.'

'Bad luck!' said Jim. Then he went over to the cupboard and came back with a pair of kitchen scales, the kind that have two sides and balance in the middle. He banged them down on the table. He pushed down on one side. 'Here's you, falling out with Rob, perhaps being threatened by him.'

Then he banged down on the other side. 'Here's Tim, a kind lad, who could be a good friend, instead he's being made fun of and treated cruelly. And it won't get any better unless you do something. Which side wins, Will boy?'

So, the same day, William went to the headteacher and told him exactly what was going on. The headteacher was mortified. 'I should have known!' he said, 'We've all let Tim down badly.'

He thanked William, and told him he had done the right thing. William was relieved, it was a load off his mind. He was still scared, though.

But do you know, none of the bad things happened. Rob didn't utter a single threat. He went very quiet for a long time.

Andy, Geoff and Simon split away from Rob and stayed friends with William. They hadn't really liked what was going on, and they knew William had done what they should have done – William was the one who'd had the courage to speak out.

William was a much happier boy in school after this. He was more confident with himself. He knew he had done the right thing once, and he could do it again.

Speaking up about bullying

Tim was much happier too, and found some real friends – and everyone in school became much better at speaking up about bullying and dealing with it, thanks to William.

✦ Conclusion

What do we learn from this story as we look forward at the start of the millennium?

If we are to have a peaceful school, a peaceful community, a peaceful world, then we must have the courage to speak up about what is wrong.

Would you have the courage to speak up? Could you do what William did? I think you could. When there's bullying, there are always people who wish it wasn't happening. They are the ones who should speak up. Blowing the whistle can only make things better for everyone.

☀ A prayer

Lord, help us to do the right thing. Give us the courage to overcome our fears, and speak out when we see wrongdoing. Protect all those who are victims of cruelty, and help us all to see that we are all equal in your sight, all worthy of love and care and respect. Amen.

☀ A thought

There's something in all of us that can drive us to cruelty. We have to guard against it all the time, so that we can grow up to respect all our fellow creatures.

Song suggestions

'How we treat each other', *Primary Assembly Song Book*, 132

'Light up the fire', *Come and Praise*, 55

Optional follow up

Discuss bullying. Provide an opportunity for any child to disclose bullying behaviour in confidence.

What makes me sad?

Assembly 4 of 4

When big emotional events happen to someone, there's always an effect on other people. This assembly, about a separation in the family, helps children to understand that.

You will need

• nothing at all.

Taken by ....

Date ....

Given to ....

Comments

● ....

● ....

● ....

✦ Introduction

In today's assembly, we'll see how someone deals with something sad that happens unexpectedly in his family. When that happens we have to think it through and try to react in a way that doesn't cause any more hurt to us or to others.

Has anything sad ever happened to you? I guess it must have. You'd be very lucky if it hadn't.

One of the very sad things that happens in lots of families is when people split up – either when married people decide not to stay together, or when someone's boyfriend or girlfriend leaves them.

Of course, when that happens, the people who are most upset are the ones who are splitting up. But other people are affected too.

In the story today, we meet Steve who sees a member of his family being really sad. It's a new experience, and it gives him a lot of things to think about.

📖 Story

Sue came home the other day. Sue's my big sister. She got married a couple of years ago, and I haven't seen a lot of her since then, because when she married Richard they went off to live a long way away, down in the south.

They had a big wedding – Sue all in white and the men in smart suits. I was one of the stars, in a sort of velvet suit as a pageboy. I have to tell you that I didn't like that suit one little bit. I did enjoy the day though. Mum made a speech, and said that she wished Dad could have been there, and she cried a bit, and so did lots of other people. Then one of Richard's pals made a speech and cheered everybody up. There was a disco afterwards, and that was good fun.

Soon afterwards, Richard had to move because of his work and, of course, Sue went with him. She found a job near where they were living.

They came home a few times. We were always glad to see them, and I was always glad to see Richard. He'd ruffle my hair and call me his mate, and I liked that a lot.

What makes me sad?

Sue would phone up Mum once a week, too. Usually she'd have a word with me as well if I was around.

And now Sue's come home again. I knew she was coming, because Mum told me. I asked her why, but she didn't have much to say about it. I knew there was something wrong – because you pick up things, don't you? From phone conversations and from the things that Mum said to other people.

I heard Sue arrive. I was upstairs on my Playstation, but I heard the door go and then I could hear Sue and Mum talking.

I was a bit disappointed that Sue hadn't called up to me, so after a bit I went down to see her.

She was sitting at the kitchen table with a cup of tea. Mum was sitting opposite her, and they were holding hands across the table. Sue had been crying.

I wanted to know what it was all about. So I just asked. 'What's going on?' I said.

Sue looked across at Mum, and Mum nodded. Sue said, 'I've decided to leave Richard.'

I had to think about that for a moment. Sue just looked at me while I was thinking. Then I said, 'Have you got divorced then?'

I didn't know much about things like that, but I did know that married people sometimes got divorced.

Sue shook her head. 'It's too soon to think about that, Steve. We might do. But at the moment I've just come home.'

I didn't feel like asking any more questions just then, so I nodded and went back upstairs. I sat with my Playstation, but I didn't play.

I just wanted to think for a bit and sort out how I felt.

I really liked Richard. From what Sue said, it seemed that I might not see him ever again. That was quite something.

I also knew from watching the telly that when people split up like that there's usually a reason for it, even though it's sometimes difficult to see the reason.

I realised that I had no way of knowing what had really happened to cause the break-up. Maybe I never would know. I thought I'd pick up bits and pieces from careful listening, like you do. But I probably wouldn't get the whole story. And Richard wouldn't be around to tell me his side of it.

But the one thing I did know was that I loved Sue. She'd been a good sister to me. She was a lot older, and she'd been a bit like another mum to me in some ways. Nothing that happened could stop me loving her, and being bothered about what happened to her.

Then I realised that Mum loved Sue of course, and she had taken Sue into the house again. So Mum must have trusted what Sue said to her. Mum wasn't going to keep going over it all, and so neither should I.

Over the next few weeks it was really difficult and really sad. Sue was terribly upset, and that made Mum upset – and that made me upset too. I just had to keep telling myself that we loved each other – Mum, Sue and me – and that was the most important thing.

What makes me sad?

All the same, I feel sad at losing Richard. I can't feel the same way that Sue feels, but I do think I've lost a friend. I'll always remember the fun we had together.

Will I see him again? Will he come to see Sue? Will Sue want to see him? It's too early to tell. All we can do at the moment is try to help each other through all of this.

✦ Conclusion

When something important happens to a person, it's a bit like throwing a pebble into a pool of water. What happens when you do that? Yes, there's a splash. And then little waves called ripples spread out across the water. One splash, but lots of effects across the pond.

In this story, Steve found that a very sad thing that happened to his sister, miles away from home, had a big effect on him. He had to think how he was going to deal with it. It brought on a mixture of feelings.

There was the feeling that he loved his sister. And that he trusted his mum's judgment.

But there was also the feeling that he missed Richard, and being upset by the thought of not seeing him again.

There was no straight answer to any of it. In the end, Steve decided that his love for his sister was the most important thing, and he would have to bear the loss of his friendship with Richard. What Steve learned from this was that he could be made very sad by something that he had no control over. Steve hadn't caused the unhappiness, and Steve could do very little to put it right. All he could do was accept it. There was no point in being angry, or finding somebody to blame. It's a hard lesson, and we all have to learn it.

☀ A prayer

Lord, we ask your help for all families where there is disagreement. Help them always to see other points of view, and to lean on the love that they have for each other. Amen.

☀ A thought

You can't solve every problem. Life sometimes brings us difficult things. But love and trust are there when you don't know what else will work.

Song suggestions

'How we treat each other,' *Primary Assembly Song Book* 66

'From the darkness came light,' *Come and Praise* 29

Optional follow up

Make a list of the things that make you sad. Then make a list of the things that you, or someone else, could do to change them. Are there any that would be difficult or impossible to change?

What makes me sad? • page 3 of 3

51

Useless

This is an assembly about a child who, while not doing well at school, finds that he is valued within his family.

You will need

- nothing at all.

Taken by	....	....	....
Date	....	....	....
Given to	....	....	....

Comments

⬤ ....

⬤ ....

✦ Introduction

Do you choose teams for playground games? People used to do it all the time. There always seemed to be two leaders who did the choosing. Nobody chose them – they just seemed to be the natural leaders. They would stand there, and all the others would stand facing them. One of them would have first pick. Who can tell me a way of choosing who would have the first pick?

Accept suggestions, such as tossing a coin.

There used to be a traditional method called scissors, stone, paper. Does anybody know it?

This is how it was done.

You have stone, which is a fist *(hold up a fist)*. You have scissors, which is two fingers stretched out *(demonstrate)*. And you have paper, which is the flat hand held out, edge towards the ground *(demonstrate)*.

What happens is that two people stand facing each other. Each has their right hand behind their back. Each brings their hand out towards each other, in the shape of either scissors, stone, or paper. You have to whip your hand out quickly, keeping the elbow into the side, both of you flicking your hands out at the same time as each other. One is always the winner because scissors cut paper, paper wraps stone, stone breaks scissors. Two the same is a draw, so you just do it again.

Who'd like to come out and try this?

You do this three times, for the best of three (remember two the same doesn't count). The winner gets to have the first choice of people for the team.

The trouble with picking people for teams is that some people are always last to be picked. The writer of this story was probably like that, because he's written a very good story about it.

📖 Story

'Oh, please let one of them choose me,' Peter said silently to himself as Lesley Merridew and Chris Burke picked the teams for the Thursday soccer match. The boys and girls were standing in a rough circle, stamping their feet and running, knees up and down, on the spot as it was chilly in the damp air of the late spring day.

'Hurry up, everyone!' That was Miss Moore, their teacher. 'Get a move on. It's too cold for dawdling.'

Useless

The number of boys and girls who were as yet unselected was down to half a dozen. Peter's inner thoughts pleaded once more, 'Not last again this week. Not last!' But his plea went unanswered – even the utterly useless Soggy Simmonds, who couldn't catch the ball and kept falling over, was chosen, and only Peter remained as Lesley's last player. Then Lesley said to Chris, 'You can have him,' and Chris refused! The others all laughed – and to give Miss Moore credit, she shut them up. Poor Peter; he had always been last to be picked, but now he was being given away! To be no use was bad enough, but to be seen as an actual handicap was the final straw. He struggled to hold back his tears.

'Where shall I play, Lesley?' he asked.

'Does it matter?' Lesley answered.

Life for Peter had always been like this, it seemed to him. In maths tests, when they'd marked the twenty mental questions and the teacher called the scores in descending order, starting with twenty, and you raised your hand when she reached your score, Peter's hand always went up near the end, often at the end. Sometimes he was so ashamed he just didn't put it up at all. It was made worse by the fact that all the others seemed to be good at something – Soggy Simmonds, for example, was a brainbox. It was always twenty out of twenty for him, so that made up for not being good at games.

But Peter didn't seem to have any one thing he was good at. Oh, in some things he was not too bad – art, for instance, and he found speaking French quite easy while others giggled and were embarrassed. But there was nothing, absolutely nothing at all, where he could with honesty say he was good, let alone best.

'Why don't you join the Cubs?' Mum said.

'They do lots of nice things and they go camping in the summer.' So he did join and for a time he enjoyed himself a lot. He found the games they played were more for fun than for real and he found he could tie knots without too much trouble. He even began to get a few badges on his arm, but not as many as the others seemed to get. When he tried some tests they often said, 'Go away and practise a bit more, Peter, and come back in a month or two.' And he knew what that meant – it meant he wasn't good enough.

'I think I'll drop out of Cubs, Mum,' he said.

'Oh, that's a pity, dear,' she answered, a bit absentmindedly as she was helping Matthew with his homework at the time.

Homework! That was another thing that showed him up. Brother Matthew and sister Marie were older and had piles of the stuff to do every night, so Peter got the chance to look at their books, and they were horrendous! So complicated! Full of the most awful gobbledegook. And in a year or so he would be expected to be able to do such work! Never!

The thought of a future filled with things that got increasingly difficult made Peter even more depressed. He might just be able to put up with being useless today if he was allowed to believe that tomorrow would be better, but it wouldn't be. It could only get worse. It was like having a toothache that refused to go away however many times you went to the dentist.

Nothing, it seemed to him, could make life worse. But then Gran got ill. Dear, lovely Gran, who Peter loved especially of all his relations. 'Not Gran!' he cried. 'Why Gran? Why not Uncle Billy who is bad-tempered and sarcastic. Or the ghastly Wayne, my slimy cousin who whines and tells tales on everybody, especially me!'

Useless

He went to visit Gran. She was in bed. 'Poor old Grannymiff!' he said to her, giving her a squeeze and a kiss which he knew she liked. 'Grannymiff' was a left-over from when he was little and hadn't been able to say 'Smith'.

'My boyfriend!' Gran said. 'That's what you are. When are you going to take me to the pictures and cuddle me in the back row?'

When Gran came out of hospital after her operation it was the summer holidays. She needed to stay in bed to recover. 'The word is convalesce,' she told Peter. 'It means I'm going to have a good long rest for the first time in my life. They've told me I mustn't get up, not for anything.'

'Not for anything?' Peter asked.

'Not for anything.'

'Not even for...'

'No, not even for that!' she laughed her great big laugh. 'I shall have to use a bucket!' But actually she had a nurse come in twice a day to wash her and do all the difficult bits, so she never needed the bucket. But she did need a lot of other things and Mum was kept busy all day and every day until she was worn out.

'You're doing too much,' Dad told her. 'You'll end up in bed yourself with nervous exhaustion. Let someone else do it.'

'And who might "someone else" be?' Mum enquired, a bit snappily because she knew there was no one else.

Dad said, 'Leave it to me.'

That evening, when, by some miracle, all the family was for once having tea at the same time, Dad said, 'Look here, you kids, there's a problem. You know how Gran is, how she needs to stay in bed, how she needs waiting on. Well, it all seems to be falling on your mother and

she's getting tired and fed up with it.'

'We do our share,' said Marie.

'We need more than that,' Dad replied. 'We need someone to be with Gran all the time. To be around the place in the daytime and to sleep there at night in case she wants anything.'

'I'll do that,' said Matthew. 'I'd like to do it.'

'Me too,' offered Marie. 'I can do my revising in peace and quiet.'

'Just hold your horses!' said Dad. 'I went round to see Gran and asked her what she thought about the suggestion. She reckoned it was a great idea ... as long as she could pick who was to do the job. And she's picked ... Peter!'

Peter moved in that evening with his toothbrush and pyjamas. Marie brought dinner round for him and Gran and the pair of them ate it together on trays in her bedroom. Dad had put up a single bed across the foot of Gran's bed and when they were both tucked up for the night they had a song-swap where Peter sang one song and Gran sang the next. They were still at it an hour later when Mum popped round to tuck them both in.

'It sounds worse than the cats outside on the roof,' she said, and you could hear from her voice that the strain on her had already lifted. 'Now, get to sleep, both of you.'

'Goodnight, Gran,' said Peter.

'Goodnight, lover boy,' said Gran. 'How about climbing over here and giving me a kiss before we drop off?'

So Peter did just that. 'Number one at last,' he smiled to himself as he closed his eyes and prepared to dream about Thunderbirds.

Peter wasn't number one at games or at some of his school work, but he was number one with his Gran.

✦ Activity

Let's try putting some people in order. Who'll come out and help me?

Let about eight to a dozen pupils come forward, from different age groups. Stand them in a line.

Now, who'll come and put these people in order of size?

Choose a volunteer to do this.

Now, let's try and put them in order of age. *(Do this with the help of the pupils themselves.)* Is it the same as size order?

Now, can we put them in order of hair colour, from darkest to lightest?

We can do this fairly easily. We might even be able to put them in order of who's best at maths, or at gym, or at playing the recorder. But we're not going to do it, because it wouldn't be very fair.

We could not, though, put them in order of who is kind, or who is very friendly, or who is very cheerful, because it all depends on who is doing the choosing.

And yet each one of these people is very precious to somebody. Each one is number one to somebody. It might not just be their families either. You sitting down there might have your best friend up here, and you think that they are number one for you.

What I want you to know is that every single one of you sitting here is precious to God. God doesn't line you up and pick some before others. He picks you all at the same time.

He doesn't worry about the colour of your hair, or how tall you are, or whether you are black or white, or whether you can play the recorder or not. You are all precious human beings, loved by Him.

☀ A prayer

Dear God, I'm a bit of a mixture, like everybody is – some bits are not too bad, others are awful. Mostly I try to be good in the way I behave and improve myself as much as I can, but still in most things I'm just sort of average. Help us to make the very best of what talents you have given us. But even if we can't do well, we are still precious in your sight. Sometimes when we're feeling miserable, we might forget that. Help us to remember it. Amen.

☀ A thought

We each have a different selection of talents, some more, some less. Some lucky ones have loads of them and seem to be able to do anything they want with no trouble at all. Others have lots of hassle, lots of grief, and need to try ten times harder to get only half as good a result. But our aim should be not to be as good as the best, that's hardly possible, but as good as we can be. Eventually, as we grow, we will find the things that we are good at, that other people cannot do. We will learn to concentrate our efforts on the things we do well. The clue to all this lies in that word 'effort'. Without effort no one gets to be as good as they could be.

Song suggestions

'The Ink is Black', *Someone's Singing Lord*, 39

'The Building Song', *Alleluya*, 59

'God Knows Me', *Come and Praise*, 15

Friendships come and go

Assembly 2 of 4

This assembly is about how friendships can cool off. Two boys gradually develop other interests, and learn how to tackle the changing relationship.

You will need

- nothing at all.

Taken by ....

Date ....

Given to ....

Comments

● ....

● ....

● ....

✦ Introduction

What's the most important thing you learn in school do you think? Is it reading? Maths?

Perhaps so. But I always think of a famous book called 'Goodbye Mr Chips', which is about a schoolmaster that everyone liked.

He thinks about all the things the school has taught its pupils and he says, 'Perhaps we taught them to get along with each other.'

He thought that was important. And I think it's important too.

The friendships you build here in school may not last forever. But in them you will learn about friendship and what makes it tick. That will stand you in good stead for the rest of your lives.

Now think for a moment. See whether what I am going to say fits you.

You have some good friends and you have people that you know and like, but you can't say they are special friends.

There are people around who used to be special friends, but now they are not really special any more. You haven't quarrelled or fallen out. You've just moved on and changed a bit.

Perhaps that's happening to you just at this moment.

Perhaps you have a special friendship and it's starting to change.

You want to do different things or your friend wants to do different things. It can be upsetting when that happens.

It's important, though, to accept that changes like that do happen. You don't have to fall out or quarrel.

Changes do happen and you have to try to accept them, as Nathan and Will did in this story.

📖 Story

Nathan and Will were always together.

They started school together in the Reception class and, as they moved up through the school, they grew closer.

Friendships come and go

They were made for each other in a way. Will was cheerful, outgoing, full of laughter and fun. Nathan was quieter, but he had a good sense of humour and he liked to listen to Will and also to feed him with good lines now and again.

They didn't always sit together in school. Their teachers sometimes deliberately kept them apart, because they did like to chat – well Will did most of the chatting, while Nathan listened and smiled.

They were together though on the playground, in assembly and in lessons where they could sit or stand where they wanted.

They were always partners in PE, always one behind the other in the dinner queue.

They spent a lot of time together after school too – at Will's house on his computer or down at the swimming baths on Thursday evenings and Saturday mornings with Nathan's dad.

Each year, they would go on holiday together. Either Will's family would take Nathan or Nathan's family would take Will.

Then, in no time at all, it was the beginning of Year 6 – the last year in the juniors.

Already all the children in the year group were starting to talk about secondary school.

On the horizon, there was a lot of change.

Will felt quite unsettled at the beginning of Year 6.

Somehow, his cheerfulness and chattiness didn't always seem right. There was seriousness in the air and he sensed the need to think about the future a bit more.

Nathan started to change too.

Will saw that change. Will would look across at Nathan and instead of looking up and grinning, or waving, Nathan would have his head in his book or he would be chewing the end of his pencil and having a good think.

Sometimes, after school, Nathan would go home on his own instead of walking with Will as he had always done before.

He didn't ignore Will.

He would say, 'Got to hurry home, Will. See you in the morning!'

Off he would go, leaving Will feeling a little bit down.

Eventually Will found out that Nathan was getting a lot more serious with his swimming and had joined a club with special sessions when the pool closed to the public.

'But we could still go on Thursdays and Saturdays with Dad,' he said to Will when he told him, but he didn't really sound all that keen to do that.

So Will decided not to go swimming any more.

During the summer holidays that year, he had met up with a friend of his dad's who ran a marching band.

He had thought about trying it, but he had hesitated because rehearsals were on Thursday afternoons and Saturday mornings.

Once Nathan started his special swimming, Will decided to go to the band rehearsals.

He found that he really enjoyed it – the instructors were teaching him to play a glockenspiel, and he really liked the marching and the fancy uniform.

Friendships come and go

By October, the two friends were really not seeing much of each other at all.

Somehow, they didn't team up as much in PE and the other lessons.

Quite often, Will or Nathan would turn round in the dinner queue to see the other one some way back talking and laughing with other people.

They didn't fall out. It wasn't like that at all. Yet both of them felt a bit – well, discontented.

Nathan talked to his dad about it when they went for some chips after swimming one night.

His dad brought it up. 'What's happened to Will these days? We should start thinking about next year's holiday soon.'

Nathan shrugged his shoulders and said, 'I miss seeing Will, but we just seem to do different things now.'

'Had a row?' asked his dad.

'Oh, no!' Nathan shook his head. 'No row. We just seem to be – well, different somehow. I feel a bit unhappy about it – sort of empty somehow, sometimes.'

His dad nodded. 'It's called growing up, Nathe,' he said. 'Time moves on, things change and people change. You've had some great times together, but now there are new things to do, new feelings inside, new people to be with.'

'Like the boys and girls in the swimming club?' asked Nathan.

'Like them,' replied his dad.

'And what about Will?' asked Nathan.

'You'll still be friends,' said his dad. 'You'll talk and laugh, and be together when it seems right or when there's a chance. Perhaps you won't be quite such special friends any more, but there's nothing wrong with that. We all go through that.'

Strangely enough, Will had a similar talk with his dad at about the same time, with the same sort of result. Perhaps it wasn't so strange, though, because the two dads often saw each other at work.

So it was that the following week, Will and Nathan met up on the school drive on the way home.

'Hi, Nathe!'

'Hi there, Will!'

They chatted for a while, both feeling a bit awkward, because they had not had a proper talk for a long time.

Then Will asked Nathan about his swimming club, and Nathan's eyes lit up and he told Will all about his times, his improvement and his coach and new friends.

Will listened and then he told Nathan about the marching band, his instrument, the marching movements, his uniform, the director and his new friends.

They both laughed and were relaxed with each other. For about a quarter of an hour, it seemed like old times.

Then they parted, quite naturally, and went their separate ways.

Both boys felt much better – it was as if something that had not been quite right had been tidied up and put properly in its place.

Friendships come and go

'I wonder if we'll be going on holiday together this year,' thought Nathan as he hurried home to get his swimming gear.

Then he pushed the thought aside. 'We'll have to see. We might,' he thought.

✦ Conclusion

What do you think? Do you think that Nathan and Will went on holiday together the following year?

There's no definite answer to that is there? They might have done or they might have had something different to do. A swimming course perhaps, or a marching band competition.

The point is that they have probably reached the point now where they could accept whatever happened, either way.

Friendships are like that.

Sometimes they are quite brief. Sometimes they last a lifetime.

Most often, I think they last for some time and then they sort of fade away – people move house, change schools or get interested in something else and meet different people.

If we accept what's happening, we know that there's no need to be jealous when new friendships form and old ones fade away.

There are always good times with past friends to look back on and good times with new friends to look forward to.

☀ A prayer

Dear God, we know that friendship is a gift – our friends support us, cheer us up and make us feel better about ourselves. Help us to see that friendships are not fixed, but can come and go. Help us to cope with the feelings and disappointments that come from that. Amen.

☀ A thought

Our lives are filled with change. Every change has good things in it if you look for them.

Song suggestions

He gave me eyes so I could see', *Tinder Box*, 19

'My Little Island', *Primary Assembly Song Book*, 88

Optional follow up

Choose words which reflect friendship and display them.

Friendships come and go • page 4 of 4   **59**

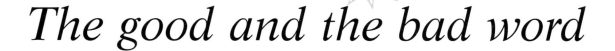

The good and the bad word

Assembly 3 of 4

This assembly is about how words are used. It shows that the same word or group of words can mean different things, depending on the context.

You will need

• nothing at all.

Taken by ....

Date ....

Given to ....

Comments

⬤ ....

⬤ ....

⬤ ....

✦ Introduction

In our assembly today we're going to think about some very powerful weapons. Not guns, not bombs or lasers. No, I mean words. Words are powerful because of the meanings they carry and the messages they bring. Words can start wars or stop them. Words can bring despair or hope or joy.

Are words good or bad? Or is it the way they are used?

What do you think? Listen to these stories.

📖 Story 1

In Wordy City, two quite aggressive words – Kick and Punch – bumped into each other.

'Ouch,' said Kick.

'Ouch yourself,' said Punch.

'You know,' said Kick, 'the trouble with you, Punch, is that you're a mean old word. You only go to work when there's trouble. "Give him a punch," they say, and there you are, all mean and nasty.'

'Oh yes?' said Punch. 'What about you? You're a violent word too, aren't you? More so, I would say. Kicking people is awful.'

Kick looked rather shocked. 'Not at all. I'm a good sporting word. "Kick it up the field," they say. "It's time for the kick off," they say. All very fair and sporting. Nothing mean and nasty at all about me.'

Punch snorted. 'Well in that case you could say the same about me. I'm all sorts of gentle things. I'm a Suffolk Punch for one thing.'

'A what?' said Kick.

'A Suffolk Punch. It's a big gentle horse. One of those big horses that works on farms and pulls carts. Nothing wrong with that.'

'Hmmm,' said Kick. 'Hardly anybody knows that. For most people, punch just means something that hurts.'

Punch shook his head.

'I'm a hole punch as well. One of those things that makes holes in paper, so you can put it in a folder. And I'm a drink. People say, "Have a glass of punch," especially at Christmas.'

The good and the bad word

Kick just sort of snorted at that, and Punch and Kick just stood there frowning at each other.

'We're always having this argument,' said Kick.

'So we are,' said Punch. 'I suppose the real answer is that it's not words that are good and bad. It's the way people use them.'

📖 Story 2

There's an old saying that goes, 'Sticks and stones may break my bones, but words can never hurt me.' It's easy to see what this means – words don't actually bruise you. All the same, I can't help thinking that whoever first said it must never have experienced being hurt with words.

You know as well as I do that you can be hurt by words – perhaps not physically hurt, not cut or bruised, but hurt all the same. Mind you, it's not actually the words that hurt, it's the way they're used. The next stories I'm going to tell you are about a note. The notes in both stories carry much the same words, but they mean very different things.

* * * * * * * * * * *

Tim was trying to remember something.

He had a terrible memory. 'You would forget your head if it were loose, Tim,' his dad would say. 'You'd forget your whole body. There'd just be your voice and the smell of your feet coming in after school, and you'd have left everything else behind.'

Tim knew he was supposed to remember something today, but he couldn't remember what it was he was supposed to remember.

He sat in class with a frown on his face. His teacher smiled, because she had an idea what was troubling him.

Right at the end of school she called Tim to her desk and said, 'Tim, your dad said to give you this note. He knew you'd forget, so I was to give it you right at the end of the day.'

Tim looked at the note, in his dad's handwriting.

It said, 'We're coming to get you after school. Don't forget!'

Tim's frown turned into a smile. That was it! That was what he couldn't remember! His dad and his Uncle Ben were picking him up after school to go and fetch Uncle Ben's new Ford Focus.

His face lit up.

That was one note. It cheered Tim up. Now listen to the story of the second note.

* * * * * * * * * * *

Nadia was feeling miserable. She was in the dining room at school, sitting all on her own, just playing with her dinner and not eating much of it, because she wasn't very hungry.

On the other side of the room sat Sarah with her two or three followers. Nadia tried not to look at them, but they stared at Nadia.

Nadia knew what they were doing. They were staring and giggling.

Soon Nadia noticed that Sarah was writing a note on a piece of paper.

She flushed red because she knew what was coming next.

Sarah's friends leaned over to read what Sarah was writing and they all giggled again.

The good and the bad word

Sarah passed the note to the next table and it made its way across the dining hall, until someone passed it to Nadia.

She opened it.

'Remember, Nadia,' she read. 'We're coming to get you after school. Don't forget!'

Nadia bit her bottom lip and started to cry.

Do you think those words were hurtful? Do you think Nadia would have been comforted if someone had said, 'Sticks and stones may break my bones, but words will never hurt me'? I don't think so. There are plenty of people here who know that words can be hurtful.

✦ Conclusion

Our story about Wordy City showed how the meaning of words, and the effect they have, actually depends on the way they are used.

In our second story about Tim and Nadia, their notes had exactly the same words, but their meaning was quite different. The way the words were used was quite different.

One of the psalms in the Bible says, 'Let my words and my thoughts always be acceptable to God.'

That's a good thought to live by. If your words and thoughts are acceptable to God, then they'll be acceptable to the people you speak to.

☀ A prayer

Dear God, the gift of language is precious. Words are wonderful and very powerful things. Help us to use language in a way that makes people feel better and not worse. Remind us of how wrong it is to use words to bully and hurt other people. Amen.

☀ A thought

Words do hurt people. They cause hurt inside, and scars that take a long time to heal.

Song suggestions

'Torch of love', *Primary Assembly Song Book*, 43

'Don't call me names', *Primary Assembly Song Book*, 63

Optional follow up

The assembly is about the values that we attribute to words. An optional way to extend this assembly is to consider what we mean by 'bad' language – are the words bad or is it the way they are used? What is swearing? This kind of discussion can be useful when there has been a problem with bad language in class or in school.

Starting with a foster family

Assembly 4 of 4

This assembly is about the sudden arrival of a foster child in a family. It explores the feelings on both sides when something like this happens. It helps children to see that life can deal harsh blows, but that there are usually people around to take some of the pain away.

You will need

• nothing at all.

Taken by ....

Date ....

Given to ....

Comments

○ ....

○ ....

○ ....

✦ Introduction

Today's assembly shows us what happens when a foster child arrives in a family in the night. We will see how the kindness of the family help the child to get over a very difficult time of worry and anxiety.

What would you do if there was a knock on the door and there was someone standing there holding a little boy's hand? What would you think if it turned out that the little boy was coming to live with you for a while?

Now some of you may know exactly what that feels like, but lots of you will not. What I'm talking about here are the families who have volunteered to be foster parents – who have decided to take on the responsibility of looking after children who, for one reason or another, have no homes of their own, or if they do have homes are not able to go back to them for some reason.

Sometimes it's just temporary – the child needs to be looked after for a while because a parent is ill and there is no one else to care for the child. Sometimes, fostering goes on for a long time.

It's not the same as adoption. When someone is adopted they become definitely part of the family – your new parents are definitely your parents, not your foster parents.

When someone is fostered they are lovingly cared for, but the arrangement isn't for ever, although it can go on for a long time.

Let's listen to a story about Sanjay and his first day with a foster family.

📖 Story

Everyone was quiet in the car as it made its way along the bypass. Mrs Roberts, the social worker, was in the front beside the driver, and Sanjay was sitting in the back looking through the window.

His mind was in a turmoil. He knew something dreadful had happened at home, and he had to be taken temporarily into care.

Starting with a foster family

Everyone said it was just for a short time, but he was just so bewildered that he didn't know what to think. Mrs Roberts had said he was going to someone's house to stay with a nice family.

Mrs Roberts turned round in the front seat and looked at Sanjay. 'Alright?' she said, and smiled. Sanjay nodded and tried to smile back, but it was difficult. He turned to look out of the window again, at the dark and rainy night outside.

* * * * * * * * * * * *

After a while the car turned into a street of houses and stopped outside what looked like quite a small house. The lights were on, and as the car drew up the front door opened, and there was a lady standing in the doorway.

Mrs Roberts got out of the car and opened the back door – 'Come on, Sanjay,' she said. 'This is it! Come and meet the Rileys.'

Mrs Roberts led the way up the drive. She spoke to Mrs Riley. 'Hello, Sandra,' she said. 'This is Sanjay. It's so good of you to take him in at such short notice.'

'Well,' said Sandra, 'I've not done it for a while, what with moving house and having my new baby and everything, but I couldn't turn you down really, when you told me about this young man.'

Then she held her hand out to Sanjay. He took it and shook it quite politely. Sandra held on to his hand and gently led him into the house. Mrs Roberts followed.

Sandra looked at Sanjay. 'You must be hungry. Steve's in the back doing some chips and fishfingers. We'll all sit down and have some in a minute.'

Mrs Roberts shook her head. 'Not me. I must be getting back. I'll be in tomorrow to see how you're all getting on.'

She put her hand on Sanjay's shoulder. He turned round, and she could see tears in his eyes. 'Don't worry, Sanjay,' she said. 'You'll be OK here till everything is sorted at home. Try not to fret. And eat your supper.'

While she was leaving, and Sandra was seeing her off at the door, a man came bustling in carrying a tray with plates of food. 'Ah! You must be Sanjay!' he said. 'Come on! I don't care what time of the night it is, I can always eat chips. Especially with bread and butter and some brown sauce. Sit up to the table then!'

Sanjay sat down, with a plate of chips and fishfingers in front of him.

Steve had some too, and Sandra had just a few chips on a small plate. 'I simply can't eat lots of chips,' she said. 'But any excuse will do for Steve.'

Sanjay sat looking down at his plate, but he didn't start eating. Sandra looked across at Steve, then spoke to Sanjay. 'Not hungry? Just eat what you can. You don't have to if you don't want to.'

Sanjay tried to eat a few chips, but he was all churned up inside, and he found it difficult. He felt he was a stranger in someone else's house. He'd never felt like that before, and it was very difficult to cope with.

'Come on, Sanjay,' said Sandra. 'I'll show you your bedroom and the bathroom. Everything's ready for you, there's even some pyjamas. I expect you didn't get a chance to bring any with you.'

Sanjay lay awake for a long time that night. If anyone had asked him how he felt, he

Starting with a foster family

wouldn't really have known what to say – except that it wasn't a good feeling. He felt numb, really – empty inside. He cried a bit, and eventually dozed off to sleep.

Next day, Steve got him up and sorted him out with having a shower and finding his clothes. 'Come down for your breakfast with us when you're ready,' he said.

When Sanjay came down, he stood for a moment at the door.

The family didn't see him at first. A big teenage girl was putting make-up on in front of a mirror. Sandra had a toddler on her knee. Sandra was eating toast and the toddler had a banana in her hand.

On the other side of the table was a little boy of about five, sitting on a chair and tucking in to a big bowl of cornflakes. Over by the sink, Steve was filling a kettle with water. They were all talking and laughing at once – or so it seemed to Sanjay – and they seemed so happy.

'I don't belong here,' Sanjay thought to himself. 'How do I fit in here? I'm not part of this at all.'

And tears started up in his eyes again.

At that moment, Steve saw him. 'Come in, Sanjay. Sit down there and see what's for breakfast. There's some toast on the table.'

Sandra turned round and took a look at him. Then she said, 'Hey, Sanjay, just the person. Sit down here.'

Sanjay sat down and looked around, the little boy just stared at him with his spoon in his hand.

Then to his surprise, Sandra plonked the toddler on his lap and he had to be quick holding on to her.

'This is Ruby,' she said. 'Persuade her to eat that banana, and then help her with her rice crispies. I'm going to finish getting dressed.'

The teenage girl turned round and smiled. 'You'll be OK with Ruby' she said. 'She likes anybody really. Now I'm off to work. Bye!'

Luckily, Sanjay knew how to manage toddlers – he had often helped with his young cousins when he lived in London. (And luckily, Sandra knew that all the time.) He jiggled Ruby on his knee for a bit and talked to her, and she looked at him with her big eyes.

The little boy watched for a bit, then he said, 'That's my little sister Ruby and I'm George. What's your name?'

Sanjay said, 'Hello, George. Hello, Ruby. My name's Sanjay.'

'Have you come to live with us?' asked George

Sanjay nodded slowly. 'For a bit, I think.'

'Good,' said George, and started on his cornflakes again.

Sanjay still felt awkward, but Ruby liked him, and he knew he could cope with giving her some breakfast. And George was quite unconcerned.

There was still sadness inside, but the sharp edge of the hurt was going away.

Steve leaned forward at the sink to catch Sandra's eye in the other room. He winked at her, and she put her thumb up.

© pfp 2002 ISBN 1 874050 56 2 May be photocopied for use only within the purchasing institution **pfp**, 61 Gray's Inn Road, London WC1X 8TH

Starting with a foster family

✦ Conclusion

Can you try to imagine Sanjay's feelings?

In the car, going to an unknown destination, he must have been filled with all kinds of fears and worries. What he needed above all was a warm welcome, and a feeling of belonging.

How did his new foster family manage to do that for him? Well, for a start, they didn't fuss him too much. They made sure he had something to eat, and a comfortable bed. He didn't sleep very well, but he was safe and warm.

Then, next day, they just brought him into family life without making a big thing of it. Sandra dumped the baby in his lap – that was really sensible, because it gave Sanjay someone else to worry about, and something useful to do. No one could take away all of Sanjay's fears and troubles, but the family did manage to make him feel a bit better.

It's so important to every one of us that we have somewhere we belong – a place and a group of people where we feel welcome and comfortable. For almost all of us, the place where we belong is our home, and the people who make us feel welcome and comfortable are our own family.

But sometimes, for some people, that goes wrong. We've seen so many examples on the television of people driven from their homes or separated from their families, so that great sadness and emptiness come into their lives.

It's important to know, though, that there are many family tragedies and sadnesses happening all the time that are never seen on the TV. Things happen to split families up, and when that happens, it's sometimes necessary for people to try hard to fit in somewhere else, with different people.

Sanjay has had terrible luck, but he has found somewhere to stay for just a while until things sort themselves out and he can go back home, which he will quite shortly.

☀ A prayer

Lord, help all families where there is trouble and tragedy. Give them strength to see it through, and may they find good friends and supporters to help them. Be with anyone here who faces a troubled time, and give us all the strength and understanding to offer them our love and support. Amen.

☀ A thought

Kindness to strangers is one of the great gifts that human beings can bring to their daily lives.

Song suggestions

'Share and share alike',s *Primary Assembly Song Book*, 72

'The family of man', *Come and Praise*, 69

Summer days

Assembly 1 of 4

This is an assembly about family holidays. It recognises the importance of rest and recreation and refers briefly to the Bible's words on this subject.

You will need

- **Optional** some holiday brochures.

Taken by	....
Date	....
Given to	....

Comments

● ....

● ....

✦ Introduction

Soon it will be holiday time for many families.

Optional *Hold up the holiday brochures.*

Some families will go off on long journeys – to the Caribbean, to Florida, to Australia. Others will go to places nearer home.

Some families may give it a miss this year because there are other things to spend the money on.

It's important, though, that everybody has a break of some kind – even if it's just a change in routine or the occasional trip out.

The Bible tells us of the importance of recreation.

Right at the start of the Bible, there is the story about the making of the world, where God rested on the seventh day.

The Bible says, 'By the seventh day, God finished what he had been doing and stopped working. He blessed the seventh day and set it apart as a special day, because by that day he had completed his creation.'

From that time, the Sabbath day has been a day for rest and for God – away from work, away from worry, away from tiredness and stress.

God wants us to rest and relax. He wants us to take care of our bodies and minds, and keep them healthy.

And our modern lives are so filled with work and worry that a longer rest in the summer is very important.

Think of your families at home.

Do the people in your family work hard during the year? Do they deserve a rest and a lie down in the sun? Of course they do.

Let's pray that they are able to have one. Like this family in my story.

📖 Story

'Right!' said Dad. 'This year we are going on holiday!'

Nick and Lindsey looked up in surprise.

Their mum kept very calm.

Summer days

'Oh yes?' she said. 'And where are we going? Bali? California? The North Pole? The planet Jupiter?'

Nick and Lindsey laughed. They knew very well what Mum was driving at.

They had not been on holiday – not a proper holiday, staying away from home together – for a long time. Not since they were both almost too young to remember.

There just wasn't enough money coming into the house.

Dad had lost his job at the pit when it closed before Nick was born. For as long as the two children could remember, he had been in a succession of casual jobs – minicab driving, security work.

Mum kept going in a twilight job at the supermarket.

They managed well enough, but everything they earned went on keeping the home together and putting food on the table.

Occasional trips and days out, yes. Holidays, no.

Nobody worried too much about it.

Nick and Lindsey had been away with their school to an outdoor centre a couple of times.

They heard other children talking about going to Disneyworld, but things like that were out of reach – like something on the television.

Most of their friends were in the same situation as them anyway. They had grown up in a town with boarded-up shops and people with very little to do.

They couldn't remember what the older people could remember – a prosperous, cheerful place, dominated by the pit at the end of the main street.

'We don't need a holiday,' said Mum. 'We're perfectly OK as we are.'

But Nick and Lindsey knew that of all of them, it was their mum who really did need and deserve a holiday.

She was always tired.

She did without nice clothes so the rest of the family could have them.

She trailed to and fro on the bus looking for the best bargains in the food shops.

'I just long to see your mum lying on the beach,' said Dad one day to Lindsey. Lindsey was surprised to see a little tear in the corner of his eye.

So Lindsey knew that her dad had spent a whole year putting small amounts of money away specially for 'Mum's holiday'.

'Don't tell her now!' he had said. 'It's a surprise. Every time I get some tips on the minicab, do a bit of overtime or do an odd job for somebody, I'll put the money in a special building society account. And we won't touch it, because nobody else will know it's there.'

Then came the day when Dad came in at teatime and said, 'Right! This year we are going on holiday!'

Mum hadn't believed it. But Dad had pulled the building society book out of his pocket and put it on the table in front of Mum.

Lindsey watched her carefully, because she was in on the secret.

Her mum picked the book up and opened it. She spent quite a few seconds studying it.

Then she looked up. Lindsey noticed that it was her turn to have a tear in the corner of her eye.

Finally, she said, 'Jack. You are a bad man. I could do all sorts with this money. Our Nick needs a new coat. Lindsey could do with some shoes.'

Lindsey spoke up. 'No Mum. It's for your holiday. You're going to lie on the beach.'

'So love,' said Dad. 'Where do you want to go?'

They sat around the table making plans. There wasn't a lot of money, so it would have to be a modest sort of holiday.

'We'll go to a caravan,' said Mum. 'We'll go to Christchurch in Dorset, where I used to go with my mum and dad. It's not far from the beach and the New Forest. And it's a lovely little town. Oh, I've wanted to go back there for years!'

'Right!' said Dad. 'This year you're going. We're all going. We'll have a lovely big caravan and I'll make sure they save some space on the beach.'

'All we need is the sun!' said Nick. And everybody laughed.

'The sun will shine on your mum this year!' said Dad. 'Just you wait and see!'

✦ Conclusion

Rest and recreation are important.

Adults sometimes neglect themselves by not having enough time to relax.

The adults in your family work hard for you and keep the home going.

If you go on holiday this year, have some outings or even just some days of relaxation, try to do your bit by making sure that the hard workers in the family really have a rest too.

☀ A prayer

Dear God, we thank you for rest, recreation and holidays. We thank you for the opportunity to refresh our bodies and minds. We think of people who will not have a holiday this year and we ask that they might at least have some time to relax. Bless all the journeys that are made this summer and keep all travellers safe. Amen.

☀ A thought

When a family goes on holiday, each family member often wants different things. One person might want to relax. One person would prefer to go sightseeing. One person would rather visit exciting theme parks. How many families have unnecessary arguments on holiday? Try to play your part by being unselfish and by remembering the needs and preferences of others who have worked hard during the year.

Song suggestions

'We'll never get away', *Primary Assembly Song Book*, 70

'I watch the sunrise', *Alleluya*, 16

Optional follow up

Plan an ideal holiday for a member of the family or a friend. Children can use holiday brochures, find out the currency, weather, etc.

Families...

Trust

Believe

Know

Trust

Assembly 2 of 4

This assembly is about the importance of trust in family relationships. It shows that the more you trust, the more likely you are to believe what someone says – and vice-versa.

You will need

- some empty cardboard boxes

- a football in a cardboard box

- the OHT provided.

Taken by	....	....	....
Date	....	....	....
Given to	....	....	....

Comments

- ....

- ....

- ....

Before the assembly

Take one child to the hall and show him or her the box with the football in it.

Ask the child to keep the meeting secret and not to join in the assembly until asked.

✦ Introduction

In this assembly we are going to look at our families and think about the feelings that family members have for each other. Today we will consider the idea of trust, because all family members hope to be able to trust each other.

Put your hand up if you are a member of a family.

Well, that's a lot of hands. I bet if you had thought about it, every hand would have gone up, because we all have families.

They may be big or small families, they may be far away, but they are there somewhere.

Who's in your family? Just the people who live in your house? Or more people than that?

It doesn't matter really. Everyone has their own ideas about their family.

A family can be made up of whoever loves you and feels close to you. It can be everyone you trust.

Who do you trust?

Do you trust your best friend?

Do you trust the people in your family?

Family life depends on trust – on knowing that people mean what they say.

We need to trust each other in school, because we are a sort of family.

Let's play a little game to see if you trust me.

Look at the boxes for a while.

What's in these boxes?

The children will be a little puzzled and uncertain how to respond.

Do you think they are empty or do you think there's something in them?

I'll tell you. They are all empty except one.

Trust

One of them has something in it.

Now, do you believe me?

Do you believe that they are all empty except one?

I need someone to back me up.

Call the child you showed the box with the football in earlier.

Can you tell them the truth? That they are all empty except one?

Of course you can.

Can you tell them which one has something in it?

Of course you can.

Turn to the rest of the children.

Do you believe *(name of pupil)*?

Well, let's see.

Open the boxes and show them to the children. Then close the boxes again.

Now, I'm not a conjurer or a magician. So it's a straightforward question. Do you all know now that there is something in one of these boxes and nothing in the others?

Of course you do, now that you've seen it.

Before, when I told you and when *(name of pupil)* told you, you had to believe we were telling the truth.

We could back each other up, but we couldn't prove what we were saying until we opened the boxes.

Whether you believed us or not depended on how much you trusted us.

There is a connection between belief and trust.

If someone tells you something and the person who tells you is someone you trust, then you will believe him or her. Your belief will be as strong as if you really knew.

Here's a story to show you what I mean.

📖 Story

Marty's dad was going away to work.

His dad was a builder by trade and there wasn't much work near where they lived. So he decided that if he was going to be able to keep his family, then he had to go where the work was.

So one morning, he got up early and packed his suitcase.

When Marty came down for his breakfast before going to school, his dad was sitting at the kitchen table with his mum.

There was a suitcase by the back door.

'Marty,' said his dad. 'I'm sorry, son, but I have to go away. We just can't manage on the bit of money your mum gets for her work on the checkout and I haven't had any proper work for ages. So I'm going down south where there is more building going on. I have to do it.'

Marty stared at his dad. It was a bombshell for him.

Quickly, all sorts of thoughts passed through his mind – the times his dad came to see him play football at school, the talks they had at the tea table, the way his dad helped him with his homework.

Marty thought the world of his dad and here he was saying that he was going away.

Trust

'Dad!' he cried. 'You can't go. We need you here. We'll manage somehow. I'll get a paper round and we don't eat much. We'll manage won't we, Mum?'

His mum sat silently, looking down at a piece of toast on her plate.

'We can't manage, Marty.' she said. 'Your dad's right. I know how you feel and I feel the same way. But he's right.'

Marty's dad reached across and put his arm on Marty's shoulder and looked at him.

He asked, 'Do you trust me, Marty?'

Marty nodded.

His dad said, 'First, believe me when I say that I have to do this. I haven't just dreamed it up and it's not because I want to leave you. I have to do it, because it's best for us. Do you believe me?'

Marty nodded again.

His dad went on. 'I want you to know that I will phone you and your mum every evening. Every single evening. When I can, I will come home and visit. I can't promise how often, because the rail fare costs money and it depends on whether I get proper work or not. But I will come home and visit. I promise you that there will come a time when I will be back here for good and we will all be together again properly. Do you believe that?'

Marty nodded again.

• • • • • • • • • • •

Later, after his dad had picked up his case and headed for the station, Marty walked to school, feeling really unhappy.

Joe, his friend, caught up with him and Marty told him what had happened.

Joe understood, because it was the sort of thing that had happened to quite a few families in their area.

'Will he ring you and come to see you?' asked Joe.

Marty answered, 'Oh, yes. I know he will, because he said so. He will come back one day. I know because he said he would.'

That's how it was. Every evening, his dad phoned to chat with Marty and his mum.

After a month, Marty went to the station to meet his dad from the train when he came home to visit.

They had a terrific weekend, with some football and lots of talking and joking.

One lovely day, more than a year after Marty's dad had gone away, he came home for good, because things were looking up in the building trade and he had managed to get a job with a local builder.

'Told you it would happen, didn't I?' said Marty's dad as he settled in his chair with a cup of tea that first evening at home.

Marty hugged his dad and said, 'I knew you would come home.'

✦ Conclusion

Think of three important words in that story.

Put up the OHT provided.

'Trust', 'believe' and 'know'.

Marty trusted his dad. If his dad said it had to be done, then Marty believed him.

Trust

If his dad said he would ring and visit, then Marty believed him.

If his dad said that he would come home for good eventually, then Marty believed him.

Actually, Marty didn't just believe him – he knew that it would happen. He told Joe that. 'I know he will,' he said.

Marty's dad was in a special position of trust. He was trusted because he had never let his son down. He knew that and he knew that he had to do what he said he would.

Suppose he had forgotten to ring for a few evenings?

He couldn't do that. No matter what he was doing he had to say, 'Just got to go and ring home now.'

He had to phone every evening.

Suppose he hadn't bothered to visit home?

But Marty knew that would not happen, so strong was his trust.

You all know who you trust.

You know your family and your friends.

You know people like Marty's dad.

Now I have an important question for you. Are you like Marty's dad?

Does your family trust you? Do your friends trust you?

If you were to tell them something, would they be sure that it was true and that you would do what you said you would do?

To be trusted is a great honour, but you have to earn it by your actions.

 ## A prayer

Dear God, the Bible tells us about trust. It says that if we trust in God, he will give us our heart's desire. Christians believe that Jesus will not let them down. We thank you for the trust that is so important in our family lives and our friendships, and we pray that we can return that trust and be trustworthy ourselves. Amen.

A thought

Trust is not given freely. It has to be earned. It is important to have somebody you can trust. It is also important to be someone who is trusted by others.

Song suggestions

'He who would valiant be', *Come and Praise*, 44

'Family prayer', *Primary Assembly Song Book*, 85

Optional follow up

- Discuss any similar situations the children have experienced.

- Ask children to write a story in which trust – or the lack of it – is the main theme.

Please say something

Assembly 3 of 4

This assembly discusses the way in which a problem can be identified and tackled once it is put into words between two people.

You will need

• nothing at all.

Taken by ....

Date ....

Given to ....

Comments

⦿ ....

⦿ ....

⦿ ....

✦ Introduction

This assembly is going to be about the importance of speaking and listening – about explanations and understanding.

Can you feel uncomfortable and slightly worried and yet not be sure what's causing it?

I think so. It might have happened to you. You just have a general sort of uneasy feeling. You're a bit quiet and sad, but you don't really know what the reason is.

There probably is a reason, but it's hidden inside you somewhere and just needs to be brought out.

That's what was wrong with Natalie in this story.

📖 Story

It was a strange sort of feeling really. A bit like a sort of heavyiness inside. It was a feeling of sadness that sometimes made Natalie want to cry. She didn't want to talk to people much either.

'You know, Dad,' she sighed on the way to school one morning, 'I don't know what's up with me.'

Her dad looked sideways at her as they walked along.

'Your gran says that,' he laughed. 'You've heard her say it.'

Which was true enough. Natalie's gran did say, 'Oooooh, dearie me! I don't know what's up with me.'

'But that's different,' said Natalie. 'Gran does know what's up with her. She's getting old and she's got painful joints.'

With that, she stopped dead in the road and looked up at her dad. He stopped with her and he was just going to speak to her again when, quite unexpectedly, she burst into tears.

Natalie's dad bent down to her and put his arms around her.

'What on Earth is the matter, Nat!' he said.

'I don't know, Dad,' said Natalie. 'I just feel miserable and worried about things.'

Please say something

'Tell you what,' said her dad. 'Let's call in at Carlo's Caff and have a cup of tea and a sit down. It's only just down here.'

'But I'll be late for school, Dad!' sobbed Natalie.

'Don't worry,' said her dad. 'I'll go in with you. This is more important.'

So they went along the parade of shops until they came to Carlo's place. It was a little cafe with four plastic-topped tables and a counter at the back. There was a big coffee machine on the counter and you could hardly see Carlo behind it.

'Hi, Carlo,' said Natalie's dad. 'Two teas please. And we'll have some toast, eh Nat?'

Natalie nodded.

'Two toast!' shouted Carlo to his wife in the back. 'Sit down you two and I'll bring it out.'

Natalie and her dad sat with their tea quietly. Natalie was still sniffing a bit and wiping her eyes when Carlo came with the toast.

'Hey, what's up here?' he said. 'Someone crying, eh? Can't have that can we?' And he touched Natalie on the shoulder. 'You eat up. Nothing like warm toast and butter to comfort the insides I say.'

Natalie cheered up a bit and smiled, and her dad said. 'Let's think what's bothering you, Natalie. Is everything OK in school?'

Natalie nodded. She actually felt better at school than anywhere else at the moment.

'At home then?' asked her dad. 'I'm not at home as much as I ought to be, but I do m

anage to take you to school in the mornings. Your mum is busy with little Gary.'

Natalie's eyes filled up with tears again when he said this and her dad was beginning to get an idea of what the problem was.

'Is it Gary?' he asked. 'Taking up your mum's time?'

Natalie thought about this for a while, and then the thoughts started to be clearer in her mind and she began to try to explain them.

'I do love Gary very much,' she said. 'He's really beautiful and I like to play with him.'

'But you're a bit jealous of him as well?' asked her dad.

Natalie looked very surprised. 'No! I'm not jealous. I just have this lumpy feeling, especially when mum is feeding him or singing to him.'

Her dad squeezed her hand. 'It is jealousy, and it's nothing to be ashamed of. The trouble with the word jealousy is that it sounds so strong and so bad, and it can lead to strong and bad things, but it's actually quite a natural feeling. The thing is to recognise it and learn to cope with it.'

Natalie looked down at her plate and fiddled with her toast. Her dad went on.

'You love Gary and you love your mum. Your mum loves Gary and she loves you. It's a complicated set up, with some strong feelings involved. It would be a surprise if there weren't some difficulties. Did you know I was jealous of Gary at first?'

Natalie looked up in surprise.

'Yes,' her dad said. 'When Gary was so close to your mum, and all her attention was on him, I felt a bit left out. Like you, I didn't

Please say something

really recognise the feeling at first, and then I thought about it. When I did think about it, I sorted my feelings out in my mind.'

Natalie nodded.

Her dad continued, 'A baby is very, very demanding. Nature has programmed Gary that way, to make sure he survives. He demands attention with his cry – he appeals for help with his beautiful face and eyes. Evolution has made human babies like that, because if the babies survive and grow, then the human race goes on. The downside is that the demands of the baby push other people aside a little. It's natural, and we have to recognise it. Remember one thing though.'

'What's that, Dad?' asked Natalie.

Her dad smiled. 'Your mum loves you just as much as she ever did. She has enough love for all of us. Whether she always has enough energy is something else. That's where we come in. You help her a lot and she really appreciates it.'

Carlo appeared at their side. 'Finished?' he asked, picking up their plates. 'Did you like your toast. Nobody can make toast like my wife. It makes me jealous.'

✦ Conclusion

If you put a problem or a feeling into words, it makes it manageable. It pins it down so that you can understand it. It's much easier to put it into words if you talk about it with someone.

Natalie and her dad decided that the feeling Natalie was having was a form of jealousy – it sounds like a strong word, but it's a natural feeling. Jealousy is not wrong. By talking about it, Natalie learned that her feelings were natural and that she could cope with them.

All religions and beliefs know that what matters is our attitude to other people – that we do not deliberately harm them or cheat them. We may have feelings about them that are difficult to cope with, but if we think, pray and really work out how we feel, then we can begin to deal with our feelings.

☀ A prayer

Dear God, we thank you for the feelings that ebb and flow inside us. Without them we would not be human and our lives would not be interesting. Help us always to recognise our feelings, and to understand how to cope with them, so that they do not get the better of us and lead us into difficulty. Amen.

☀ A thought

Jealousy is really a lack of understanding of the needs of others. If we try to understand what other people need from us, then we are on the way to overcoming jealous feelings.

Song suggestions

'Make me a channel of your peace', *Alleluya*, 42

'How we treat each other', *Primary Assembly Song Book*, 66

Tell them how you feel

It's difficult to put feelings into words for the people who need to hear them.

Tell them how you feel • OHT

Tell them how you feel

Assembly 4 of 4

It can often be hard to make feelings known to people who deserve or need to know. And yet the ability to express feelings is one of the signs of developing emotional and spiritual maturity. In this assembly, a child who is fostered finds difficulty in showing her real feelings towards her foster parents. One day, though, she finds the right words.

You will need

• the OHT provided.

Taken by	....	....	....
Date	....	....	....
Given to	....	....	....

Comments

⦿ ....

⦿ ....

⦿ ....

✦ Introduction

Today's assembly story is about a girl who has very warm feelings towards some people but is afraid to express them aloud, until her good friend helps her.

Think of all the people close to you. How do you feel about them?

Do you love the people in your family?

Do you like the way your friend makes you laugh?

Do you appreciate how kind everyone was the last time you were ill?

Let me ask you this. When was the last time you told them how you feel?

It's not difficult to think about those feelings. What's much more difficult, though, is to put them into words for the people who need to hear.

I wonder why it's so difficult? I think it's just something about human beings that makes them a bit reserved.

And yet sometimes it's good to say these things to the people who matter in your life.

Sometimes it's not just good, it's necessary and important.

That's certainly how it was in this story, when Sarah eventually made a big decision.

Put up OHT supplied.

📖 Story

'You know,' said Sarah, 'they're not my mum and dad.'

Sarah and Janine were sitting together in Sarah's bedroom. They were supposed to be doing their maths homework together, but if the truth were known, not a lot of work was getting done.

'Well,' replied Janine, 'I think we all know that. You do call them Stan and Janet after all. And you don't look a bit like them. You're – well, different.'

'A different colour you mean?' said Sarah. 'I suppose people notice that, but I always

Tell them how you feel

forget about it. No, I call them Stan and Janet because I remember coming to them. If you're fostered or adopted when you're a little baby it's different, because you just naturally say Mum and Dad.

'But I was six when I came to Stan and Janet. The social worker said, "Sarah, this is Stan and Janet," and that's what I've called them ever since.'

'So what happened? What about your real mum and dad?' asked Janine.

Sarah shook her head. 'I don't know much. One day I might see if I can find out, but not yet.'

Janine thought for a moment.

'Sarah,' she asked, 'what's it like to be looked after by people who aren't your mum and dad?'

Sarah looked up.

'Hmm?' she said. 'Not my mum and dad? It's not like that. Stan and Janet *are* my mum and dad to me. It's no different. In fact I love them that much more really.'

'Why's that?' asked Janine.

'Because they took me in,' said Sarah.

'When I was in the children's home, the one thing I really wanted more than anything else was to be in a family, with my own room, and someone to be my mum and dad – or at least just my mum or my dad. Either would have been OK.

'I was lucky, I got both. And they chose me, remember. They didn't have to have me. They didn't have to have anybody. Or they

could have chosen someone else. But they chose me.'

'So,' said Janine. 'Why don't you call them Mum and Dad then – if that's how you feel about it?'

Sarah shrugged. 'Don't know really. I've just always called them Stan and Janet. It would seem strange calling them something else. And I'm not sure they'd like it. They're used to me calling them by their names now.'

Janine shook her head. 'I reckon they'd like it. It's special being someone's mum or someone's dad. I reckon they'd like it.'

'So why haven't they asked me to call them it then?' asked Sarah. 'If they'd wanted me to they'd have said so by now.'

Janine shook her head again. 'I don't think they would,' she said. 'I reckon they don't want to push you. And it would be awful if you said no. Suppose they said, "Call us Mum and Dad," and you said, "I don't want to." Think how they'd feel about that.'

'But I wouldn't say no,' said Sarah.

'They don't know that, silly,' said Janine. 'They don't know how you feel deep inside. For all they know you might not think of them as mum and dad. They don't want to risk having all that out and being talked about. No. It's got to come from you.'

The two friends didn't say any more about it. They got on with their homework, then came down to have beans on toast with Stan and Janet. During tea, Janine kept looking at Sarah and then at Stan and Janet, but she didn't say anything else.

Tell them how you feel

That night, in bed, Sarah thought a lot about what Janine had said. It was good to have a friend to talk about things like that with, she thought.

Janine was a very sensible girl and seemed to be very good at guessing what people were feeling and how they might react to something you said.

She decided that Janine was probably right.

The next evening, after school, Sarah spent some time plucking up courage.

She watched her favourite television programmes and had her tea with Stan and Janet, and all the time she wanted to ask them about calling them Mum and Dad. But the time never seemed to be right. They were always talking about something else.

So, in the end she chose to do it at what was quite an awkward moment.

Janet was on her way to the kitchen door with the tea things on a tray. Stan was standing up, too, ready to nip out into the garden to have a cigarette – he was only allowed to smoke outside.

Sarah said, 'Stan and Janet, can I ask you something?'

Stan said, 'Ask away, chick, we're listening.'

Sarah cleared her throat. 'Would it be alright, er… Do you think it would be OK if I called you Mum and Dad?'

She wasn't really ready for what happened then.

Oh, she had tried to think of various things that might happen. She'd sort of rehearsed them in her mind, trying to imagine what they would say to her, and how she would take it.

Sometimes she thought Stan might ruffle her hair and say, 'That's OK chick, you call us what you want.'

And at other times she even thought they might say, 'Not sure about that Sarah, love, we'll have to think about it.'

What actually happened was that there was a moment of silence. Then without a word Janet carried on into the kitchen, and Stan followed her there.

Sarah sat at the table for a moment, wondering what was going on, then she followed them into the kitchen.

She found Stan and Janet holding each other, and they were both crying. As she went in they broke away and they both held their arms out to her.

'Oh Sarah, come to your mum and dad,' said Janet. 'This is the happiest day of our lives.'

✦ Conclusion

Can you see how important it was for Sarah to put her feelings into words?

Stan and Janet wanted her to call them Mum and Dad, but they weren't going to be the first to say it, because it would have been too disappointing if Sarah hadn't been happy about it.

Tell them how you feel

They didn't want to make Sarah feel awkward about something she wasn't comfortable with. And they didn't want to feel upset themselves if she said no.

And can you see how important Janine was in this?

She was the friend who could listen carefully to someone else talking about their feelings and then give good advice – and what wise advice it was too.

There are times when it's good to put your feelings into words – to tell your family that you love them, for example.

People appreciate that – everyone likes to hear that they are loved – and it makes you grow closer together.

 ## A prayer

Lord, we thank you for the love that keeps our families together. Help us not to take it for granted, but to speak the feelings that are in our hearts and to show how much we depend on each other. Amen.

A thought

Share your feelings. Then other people benefit from them too.

Song suggestions

'Family Prayer', *Primary Assembly Song Book,* 85

'The Best Gift', *Come and Praise,* 59

Optional follow up

Do you have feelings for people that you can't express. Write them down. Keep them private. Then see if you can act on the thoughts you've written down.

Who are the people who help us?

Assembly 1 of 4

This assembly focuses on the people who help to keep any community going and tells of one of the urban projects of Save the Children.

You will need

- a large and unwieldy pile of light objects, for example boxes, papers or books

- the OHT provided and pens.

Taken by	....	....	....
Date	....	....	....
Given to	....	....	....

Comments

- ....
- ....
- ....

✦ Introduction

Carry your large and unwieldy pile of things into assembly.

Do some histrionic staggering around with them and eventually let them fall in as spectacular a fashion as you can.

Fall down yourself if you feel up to it. Get up, dust yourself down.

Put your hand up if you would like to help me pick these things up.

There will, of course, be lots of volunteers.

Choose some and together pick things up.

It's really good when people help you. There are some things that are so much easier if you have help.

I appreciate all the help I can get in my work. I do get a lot of help, too.

When I think about it, I didn't really need even to start carrying all those things that I dropped. Someone would have helped me to carry them.

Let's look at this picture.

Put up the OHT provided.

It's a school. Let's say it's our school. What's special about it in this picture?

That's right. The school is floating above the ground. It has no support.

It might fall at any minute and that would be a disaster for the teachers and the pupils.

What it needs are some strong people underneath to hold it up and stop it from falling down.

Let's put some strong people underneath.

I'll choose the first one. Here it is, it's (*name*) the caretaker.

Without (*him/her*), we would be all in trouble. (*He/she*) looks after the heating and makes sure that the cleaning is done.

(*He/she*) makes sure the school is secure and safe.

It's a demanding job and it takes a strong person.

Who are the people who help us?

So here is the strong person, helping to hold up our school.

Write his or her name on the OHT.

Now can anyone give me another strong person who supports our school?

Take suggestions, they might include secretarial staff, ground staff, governors known to the children, classroom helpers, cleaners, kitchen staff, playground supervisors and parent volunteers.

There they are – a whole team of people there to help us and to make sure that teachers can teach and that you can learn.

Each person does something important – so important that they would really be missed if they were not there. The school is well supported.

That means, of course, that we must, in turn, support and care for the people who help us.

Now let me tell you about someone who wanted to help and support children both in and out of school.

Her name was Eglantyne Jebb and she saw for herself, in 1919, what many of us have seen on television – that the people who really suffer most in wars are the children.

So often their families and homes are torn from them and they are left unhappy, sick and with no one to care for them.

'Every war is a war against the child,' she said.

So she started a charity called 'Save the Children'.

We think of Save the Children as helping people in the developing world and it does do much work there. But there are needs in our country too.

Sixty years ago, for example, Save the Children was delivering free milk to schools in areas where miners were on strike.

Work like that still goes on today.

Here's the story of Edward.

📖 Story

My mum is called Maria. I have a sister called Karen, a year younger than me.

We live in a maisonette on an estate in a place where there used to be a coal mine.

I think I can remember the coal mine, but only just, because it closed a few years ago.

My dad worked down the mine. When it closed, he couldn't get another job. My mum says he got more and more depressed and very bad tempered.

In the end, he left us and we don't see him any more.

My mum also gets depressed. She can't find a job.

It would be difficult anyway, because she has to look after me and my sister when we are home from school.

What really upset my mum was when her mum – our Nan – died last year. Mum relied on her a lot.

Nan was usually cheerful. I think she had seen a lot of troubles in her life, which meant that she could cope with things better than my mum.

She died quite suddenly and my mum could hardly speak for weeks without crying.

Then Mum started to have these really bad moods, when she would stare into space and shout at us if we spoke to her.

Who are the people who help us?

The trouble is, you see, that we don't have enough money.

My mum gets some allowances, but things are expensive.

We can't get out to the supermarkets where the bargains are. You need a car for that. We had one when my dad was working, I remember – an Escort – but I've almost forgotten what it was like to be in it.

We don't go on holiday and we don't have much in the way of presents.

That doesn't bother me too much though, because all my friends are the same. All we want is for our mums to be more cheerful.

Now, though, I am helping my mum.

I found out from one of the dinner ladies at school that Save the Children had started a drop-in centre in an empty flat on our estate.

I persuaded Mum to go, and she goes there quite a lot now. We can go too. Mum can talk to other women and share ideas and sometimes they have a cry together. Mostly they end up laughing.

We can play games and that, and there's a summer play scheme.

The latest is that mum and the other women are starting a course, which will give them qualifications to run their own playgroups.

I feel better now, because my mum feels better, and doesn't have so many bad days. I know my school work is better now, too, and my sister thinks the same about hers.

Most of all, I think the drop-in centre reminds people that we are here and that we need help. We thought everybody had forgotten us.

✦ Conclusion

So if this picture on the OHT were of the school that Edward goes to, we could add another supporter – a charity called Save the Children, which is helping families and making children less unhappy.

☀ A prayer

Dear God, we thank you for the feelings that ebb and flow inside us. Without them we would not be human and our lives would not be interesting. Help us always to recognise our feelings, and to understand how to cope with them, so that they do not get the better of us and lead us into difficulty. Amen.

☀ A thought

If we can't offer help ourselves, then perhaps we can support caring organisations.

Song suggestions

'He is there', *Primary Assembly Song Book*, 35

'A better world', *Alleluya*, 60

Optional follow up

- Find out more about the work of Save the Children.

- In class produce an image such as the 'floating school' used here for a display on the theme of 'People who help us'.

Who are the people who help us?

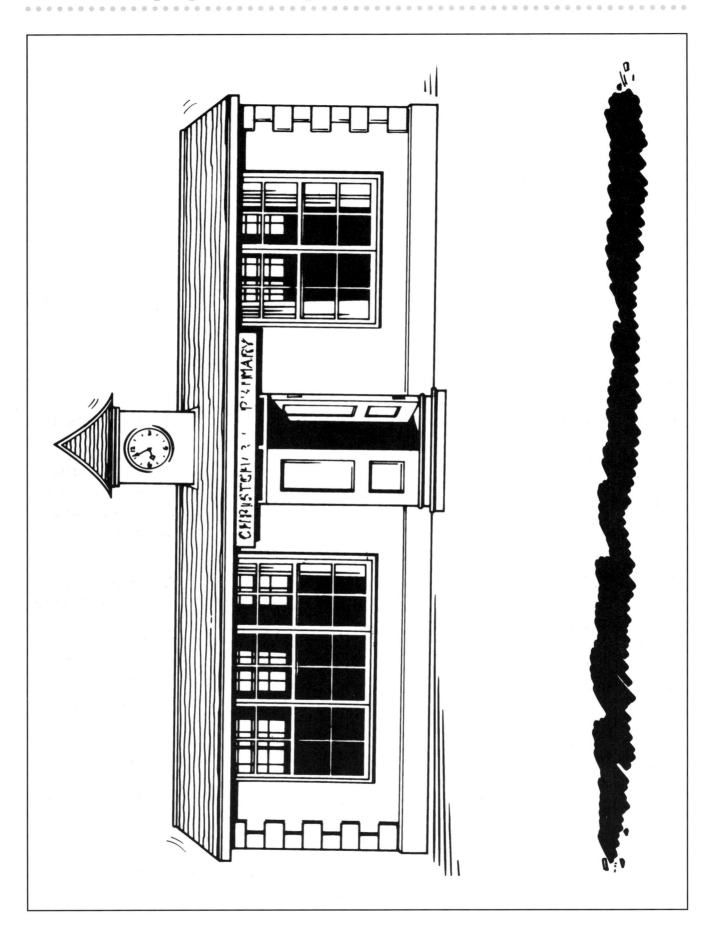

Who are the people who help us? • OHT

Emergency help

Assembly 2 of 4

This assembly is about a school that had a big problem – a fire in the night that destroyed much of the building. Based on a true story, it tells how everyone rallied round, gave support and helped.

You will need

• a blank OHT and pens.

Taken by	....	....	....
Date	....	....	....
Given to	....	....	....

Comments

● ....

● ....

● ....

✦ Introduction

Our assembly today is about what makes a school a good place to be, and the relationships and friendships that keep it all going. One real test of a school comes when there is a big problem. This true story is about such a problem.

Who has had a problem in their house – perhaps a fire with lots of smoke or a burst pipe with water all over the place?

It's not funny is it? I'm sure it was a terrible time for everyone in the house. But I am sure of another thing too – I bet there were people offering to help you.

Can you tell me how people offered to help?

Take some examples and write them on the OHT.

Listen to this story about a school that had a big problem.

📖 Story

At Mrs Harrison's house, the phone rang in the night.

Nobody likes the phone to ring in the night. It's almost always trouble – somebody in the family with a problem, a call to go to work, somebody stranded after the last bus. You never get good news in the night.

You don't hear, 'Ooh, hello, I know it's three am, but I thought you'd like to know that I've won ten pounds on the lottery!'

As it's not going to be good news, you are pretty sure it's going to be bad news.

Mrs Harrison was sure it was something to do with school.

Being headteacher meant that the phone sometimes rang in the night because the burglar alarm was ringing, and nobody could find the caretaker.

So sometimes she had to go down there and see if there was a break in and turn the alarm off.

Emergency help

That's what it would be tonight. The alarm ringing.

She got out of bed and went out on the landing. She picked up the handset of the phone and sleepily said, 'Hello.'

'It's Jim,' said the voice. She started to wake up. Jim was the caretaker. If he was ringing her, there must be a problem that he couldn't solve, which meant it was a big one.

'Yes Jim. What's up?' she asked.

'Sorry, Mrs Harrison,' he replied. 'The school's on fire.'

Mrs Harrison was so shocked that she did not speak.

Jim went on. 'It's a big one, I'm afraid. There are firefighters and engines here, and the police. Can you come?'

'I'm on my way,' she said.

· · · · · · · · · · · · ·

Thirty-five minutes later she was standing with Jim watching flames coming through the roof of her brand new library and entrance hall, while the firefighters pumped water on to it.

Tears were running down her cheeks.

She just wanted to shout and scream, it was so dreadful and frustrating.

'After all our work,' she said to herself. 'All the library books gone. All the paperwork in the office. All the teachers' work in their lockers.'

At that moment, in the dark, with the smoke, the shouts of the firefighters and the water streaming past her down the drive, she felt very alone.

'I'm not sure I can cope with this,' she thought. 'It's not quite the same as a flood in the boys' toilet, is it?'

She got out her mobile phone and rang Mr Thompson, the deputy head, and briefly told him what was going on.

'Could you get some of the others here?' she asked him.

· · · · · · · · · · · ·

By five am the fire was out.

Most of the teachers were standing with Mrs Harrison and the chief fire officer was planning to show them which parts of the building were destroyed, which were badly damaged and which had not been affected.

Obviously, school could not open that day. Mr Thompson phoned the local radio station to let as many parents know as possible and, from eight am onwards, he and two other teachers stood at the gate to tell parents to take their children home and wait for further news.

'We will only close for one day!' said Mrs Harrison. 'I don't care what we have to do.'

The front part of the school – the entrance hall, the offices and the new library – were destroyed. The hall, the staffroom and everything in them, were damaged by smoke.

But the classrooms on the other side of the hall and the mobile classrooms on the playground were not affected.

So Mrs Harrison and the teachers set to and worked out how they could run the school in the buildings that they had.

Emergency help

As the day wore on, the offers of help arrived. Every headteacher in the town called in and offered to take some pupils in.

'Thank you,' said Mrs Harrison. 'But we are staying here together!'

Then the parents started turning up. They wanted to clean up the smoke damaged rooms.

'Sorry,' Mrs Harrison had to say. 'But it has to be done by professionals. They'll be here shortly.'

Lots of the parents stayed and helped the teachers in all sorts of ways.

They helped to share out books between classes and to copy out new, temporary registers.

Then teachers from other schools arrived in cars. One brought a photocopier in the back of an estate car.

'You'll need this more than we will at the moment,' said the teacher who brought it.

Another teacher brought a kettle, two teapots, some mugs and some coffee, tea, milk and sugar.

'I guess you might need these even more than the photocopier!' she said.

'I think you're right!' agreed Mrs Harrison.

At lunchtime, a group of people from the Sikh temple turned up with containers of food for all the people on the site.

After dinner, one of the governors came with a laptop computer and a portable printer and started to do letters to all the parents.

The local newsagent range and said that if Mrs Harrison sent some letters round explaining what was happening, his paper-round workers would deliver them to his customers.

That meant that a good number of parents would get their letters.

The head of the secondary school also offered to send letters home with their pupils.

By five o'clock in the evening, Mrs Harrison had been at school for fourteen hours.

She was weary, dirty from the smoke and ready for a shower and a rest.

'Go home,' said Mr Thompson. 'We can do the rest. You be here tomorrow to welcome the children.'

She laughed. 'I feel surplus to requirements. In the night I felt so alone. Now I feel that everyone is helping me.'

Next day, after a good night's sleep, she was standing on the playground as all the children and the parents gathered.

'We've had a serious event,' she said. 'We can't deny that. But I want to say a few things.

'First, it's been wonderful to see how everyone has worked together to make the problem less serious than it might have been.

'Second, we were determined to open today. We will call your names out in a minute and you can go with your teacher. There's plenty of work to do! It's quite safe, although we won't be able to use the library, there won't be indoor PE and we will be going up to the secondary school for dinner. But we are going to do our best, all together.'

Everyone clapped loudly.

Mrs Harrison carried on.

Emergency help

'Third, I promise you that before this time next year, you will be invited to the opening of the rebuilt front part of the school, better than ever!'

Another loud cheer went up.

'Finally,' she said, 'I want to remind you that the school is you, me, and all of us. A school is not a building, it is a community of people. We could meet in a field and we would still be Marsham Primary School. So let's go in and get on with what we do best – enjoying our work in our classrooms!'

✦ Conclusion

When things go wrong, people want to help. You find out that you have real friends in unexpected places.
The best friends are those who can see exactly what sort of help you need and then get on with providing it.

Try to be that sort of friend – be there with the right words or the right actions, before you have to be asked. Try at home with your family. Try it at school with your friends.

☀ A prayer

Dear God, we ask your help for all those who have woken up to big problems in their lives this morning. We ask you to be with them, to comfort them and also to be with all those who are giving support. Give us all the knowledge and strength to be supportive friends when the need arises. Amen.

☀ A thought

The Beatles sang, 'I'll get by with a little help from my friends.' It's a very true thought – you can cope with most things with someone by your side.

Song suggestions

'With a little help from my friends', *Alleluya*, 38

'Friends', *Primary Assembly Song Book*, 83

Optional follow up

Ask a member of the emergency services to school, to talk about work in the community. Give them a copy of this assembly as preparation.

Celebrate school

Assembly 3 of 4

This assembly celebrates some of the values to which most primary schools would aspire. It builds these into a ceremony which can be used at any time, or at the end of the school year when people are moving on.

You will need

- six candles – mounted so that they can be safely handled by children when lit
- the OHT provided.

Taken by ....

Date ....

Given to ....

Comments

● ....

● ....

● ....

Note to the teacher

The assembly is written to be suitable for the end of the school year. Only slight omissions and changes will make it suitable for other times of the year.

✦ Introduction

In this assembly we are going to celebrate all of the good things that go on in our school and the people in our school who make these things happen. We will think about our values and ideas and how we can go on making things better for everyone.

Today we are going to have a celebration. What will we be celebrating? Not a birthday, although it might well be somebody's birthday. If it is, they are welcome to enjoy the celebration with us.

No, we are going to celebrate some of the good things about our school, and about our lives together here. It will remind us all of what we are here for, and build up a good memory for those who are moving on from us.

To begin, let's look at this list on the OHP.

Put up the OHT provided.

Caring for each other.

Ready to learn.

Improving all the time.

Accepting our differences.

Respecting our surroundings.

Showing concern for our world and its people.

I hope that those statements are true of every single one of us here, and that as you go through school we will have helped you to understand each of them a little better.

First, let's look a little more closely at them and I'll tell you a little story to illustrate each one.

These stories are not about anyone here, but it's easy to think of people who are very similar.

Celebrate school

📖 Short Stories

Caring for each other

I'll tell you about Matthew. He was often in trouble at school. He was a bit cheeky and one of his favourite sayings was, 'Miss! It wasn't me!'

But the great thing about Matthew was that he was really kind. His gran had brought him up and had taught him the value of caring for other people.

'I had it really hard when I was young,' she said. 'I was smaller than most of the other kids and they used to pick on me. Always think how you would like to be treated yourself and treat the people in your class like that.'

So, although Matthew was cheeky and chatted too much in class, he always knew when his classmates needed a bit of support.

He would make friends with newcomers. He would let the teacher know if someone had been crying. He would share his sweets around.

He could have worked harder I suppose, but he really was the kind of person his school and his gran could be proud of.

Ready to learn

Gina's dad had said to her, 'Gin!' (He called her that for a joke – 'Gin, you're a tonic!' he would say.) 'Gin, I didn't come to this country for me. Look at me, I'm still pushing trolleys at the hospital. I came for my kids. I don't care what you end up as, as long as you do your best. We'll support you all the way.'

So Gina was always ready to learn. Sometimes she worried about her work. Her teachers had to reassure her, and ask her dad to be understanding.

Sometimes she was a bit quiet, when she might have been asking questions, but she was determined to succeed and she knew what she was in school for.

Improving all the time

Tony found reading really difficult, and it took him quite a long time to get the hang of it.

He would look at the page and not be able to see what he was supposed to see. Great big tears would come in his eyes and roll down his cheeks.

His teacher would comfort him and put her arm round him.

'It's OK, Tony. You'll get there in the end,' she would say.

Mrs Chatterjee, the classroom helper would spend lots of time with him, but he would sometimes still get upset.

'I can't do it!' he would say and the tears would start again.

But of course, he did start to improve. He didn't even know he was improving at first, until Mrs Chatterjee showed him some words he couldn't read before and could now.

Gradually he made progress – each week a bit better than the week before.

'That's what's important, Tony,' said Mrs Chatterjee. 'Never mind what the others are doing. You're improving all the time.'

Accepting our differences

Nathalie's mum always said to her, 'Remember, Nat, that you are as good as anyone else. You can do most of the things that other people can do, and you can do lots that nobody else can do.'

So the fact that Nathalie had never been able to walk, and used a wheelchair at school, did not seem to bother her.

Celebrate school

It bothered the rest of her class when she first arrived – they weren't sure how much to help her and how much to leave her alone. Some of them made the mistake of fussing her too much. Eventually, though, with the help of their teachers, they realised that it was better to do too little than too much.

They also realised that Nathalie could get into trouble. Once she got told off for going too fast in the corridor.

'If you ladder my tights, my girl!' said Mrs Williams that day. 'I'll get your mum to stop your pocket money for some new ones.' She meant it too.

Respecting our surroundings

Sandhu went to see the headteacher one day.

'Please, Sir,' he said. 'Can we have some benches to sit on when we're outside?'

The head thought about it and asked some of the other children. Sure enough, they all felt the same way. When the weather was fine, they often just wanted to sit around and talk, or show each other books and things that they had brought to school.

So the head found some money and some good vandal-proof benches, and had them put in.

'Well done, Sandhu,' said the head. 'There'll be a special certificate for you on achievement evening.'

Showing concern for our world and its people

Joe heard a talk in church about street children in Mexico and the work that Christian Aid was doing to help them.

'That could be me,' he thought. 'I could have been homeless and begging on the street, somewhere, if my mum and dad hadn't fostered me and brought me to Britain.'

So he badgered his family, his friends and his school to put on a big jumble sale for Christian Aid. It raised quite a lot of money. More importantly, he made a lot of people think about wider problems than their own.

Each one of these children is very like somebody here. I won't embarrass anybody by making comparisons. Many of you are like more than one of them at the same time.

One important thing is that they are all different – there is room here for all sorts of people.

✦ Ceremony

Let's have six people to take part in this little ceremony of celebration.

Light the candles and take six volunteers.

To the first volunteer.

Pick up a candle and stand by me.

This small light, held by a pupil of this school, represents a part of the values we stand for. We recognise all those here who show care and concern for others, in the knowledge that we could all do better in this.

To the second volunteer.

Pick up the next candle and stand by me.

With this small light, we recognise all those here who understand the value and enjoyment of learning. May we remember that although we do many good things in school, what matters most is the way we learn in our classrooms.

To the third volunteer.

Pick up the next candle and stand by me.

Celebrate school

With this small light, we recognise all those who make progress, however small, and in whatever way, during their time here. May we always recognise progress and be constantly reminded of its importance.

To the fourth volunteer.

Pick up the next candle and stand by me.

With this small light, we recognise and rejoice in our differences. Each one of us is different from the others in all sorts of ways. It is these differences that add richness and variety to our lives. May we never be tempted to treat anyone badly because of our differences.

To the fifth volunteer.

Pick up the next candle and stand by me.

With this small light we remember how important it is to be aware of this building, its surroundings and our local community. May we always show respect for the places in which we live and work.

To the sixth volunteer.

Pick up the next candle and stand by me.

With this small light we remember the great struggle for survival that goes on across the world.

We ask that light may shine into the lives of people who are homeless, hungry or in fear, wherever they may be.

We particularly bring to mind the many children, everywhere, whose lives are filled with fear and danger.

Now I ask the candle bearers to walk slowly, in procession, out of the hall, while we keep silence. What we are showing is that these pupils, on behalf of all of us, are taking our values and beliefs with them out into the world.

Take these lights, symbols of the good things in our lives here, and carry them with you out of our hall to shine in the world outside.

Slow procession out of the hall to music if possible – guide them if you need to. Don't forget to let them back in for the rest of assembly!

Optional

We take our school for granted. Perhaps, in some ways, that's how it should be. We certainly shouldn't be thinking about school all the time, day and night. I have to stop myself from doing that!

But it's good, sometimes, just to look at ourselves, to see what's important here, to give thanks for the successes that we have, and pray for the strength and ability to do even better.

☀ A prayer

Dear God, help us to keep faith with the things we believe in. May our actions be guided by your teaching and may our lives continue to be in tune with all that we have learned in our school. Amen.

☀ A thought

Know what you stand for. Stick by your beliefs. be true to yourself and to the things you have learned.

Song suggestions

'One more step', *Come and Praise*, 47

'To build a memory', *Primary Assembly Song Book*, 49

© **pfp** 2002 ISBN 1 874050 56 2 May be photocopied for use only within the purchasing institution **pfp**, 61 Gray's Inn Road, London WC1X 8TH

★ Caring for each other.

★ Ready to learn.

★ Improving all the time.

★ Accepting our differences.

★ Respecting our surroundings.

★ Showing concern for our world and its people.

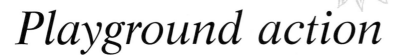

Playground action

Assembly 4 of 4

In this assembly a class of children decide to take a hand in the council's plans for their local playground. It reminds us that children have opinions worth listening to and that people who regard themselves as experts should be prepared to listen to others.

You will need

- nothing at all.

Taken by	....
Date	....
Given to	....

Comments

⬤ ....

⬤ ....

⬤ ....

✦ Introduction

Today's assembly shows us how we can all have a say in what happens in our school and our community. Adults must encourage children to contribute their ideas and opinions so that school or community can really reflect on the needs of all.

Have you ever had the feeling that nobody is listening to you? If that happens in school, then perhaps sometimes it's my fault, and I'm sorry. But in case it makes you feel better, it happens to all of us at some time.

Part of the problem is that people often don't like asking for help. If someone is an expert, then it takes courage for them to admit that they don't know everything and to ask for help – but the sign of a mature and well-balanced person is that they have that courage. They will stop and say, 'Hang on, let's ask someone else about this.'

All the same, both sides have to make the effort. Experts have to listen, people have to speak up.

This story shows both sides – a group of children who decided not to be ignored, and an expert who asked for help.

📖 Story

Miss, they're taking down the old swings and things in the corner of Dorway Park,' said Tricia before registration one morning.

'Not before time,' said Miss Fardon. 'Those things were getting dangerous. I'm surprised nobody has been hurt.'

Gurdip butted in, 'Is there going to be nothing there now? No play equipment?'

Miss Fardon pricked up her ears at that. She was always alert for a chance to involve her class in something.

'Let's find out,' she said. 'We'll write to the council and ask them if they have any plans for that bit of the park.'

So that's what they did, in a class English lesson.

Playground action

Soon there was a reply.

'Thank you for your interest. We have decided to put more up-to-date play equipment in that space.

Yours sincerely,

Fred Johnson
Director of Leisure and Recreation Services.'

Tricia sniffed. 'A bit short and sweet I think that is,' she said. 'I think if they are putting kids' things in, they ought to ask us about it.'

'That's right,' agreed Miss Fardon. 'So write and tell them so. Do it today.'

Tricia wrote on behalf of the whole class.

'Dear Mr Johnson,

We're glad you're putting some more modern play equipment into Dorway Park. But we think you ought to ask some children what they want.

We will find out for you if you like.'

⊕ ⊕ ⊕ ⊕ ⊕ ⊕ ⊕ ⊕ ⊕

Tricia's letter caused a lot of thinking and talking to go on at the Council offices.

Miss Williams from the Council said, 'I think we've made a mistake. This playground is for children. But the one thing we haven't done is talk to the children. We should do that, and be prepared to change our ideas if necessary.'

So Miss Williams went down to the school and met Tricia and Gurdip and the others.

'What I want you to do,' she said, 'is talk to lots of other children – older than you and younger as well as those of your own age.

'Try to come up with a list of ideas for the playground.'

Miss Fardon helped, and the class did a good survey of opinions, which they wrote up on the computer and presented very professionally in a folder.

Miss Williams was very impressed with it, and discussed it in a meeting with Mr Johnson and some of the other council officials.

'Well,' said Mr Johnson. 'Some of the things are what we thought of ourselves – a safe surface in case people fall, safe swings in case they hit people, a big climbing frame with lots of layers and easy and hard sections.'

'But there are unexpected things,' said Miss Williams. 'Places to be quiet, for instance – dens, really. And seats to sit on. It's clear that we have to think of this as a meeting place for children – somewhere to talk and just sit around – and not just as a play area. We've been thinking of a really colourful, active sort of place. The children want that, but they want this quieter feel to it, too. We'll talk again to the manufacturer about that.'

⊕ ⊕ ⊕ ⊕ ⊕ ⊕ ⊕ ⊕ ⊕

In the spring, the playground opened and there was a ceremony.

The people who built the playground were there, and Mr Johnson, and Miss Williams. And, of course Miss Fardon and the class were all there, too.

Mr Johnson made a speech, and said, 'I would like to thank the children in Miss Fardon's class for their help. It taught me that after thirty years working with the Council, I don't really know everything, and I have to listen.

Playground action

I'm really glad that Miss Williams agreed with me.'

And then Tricia and Gurdip stepped forward and cut a ribbon with a big pair of scissors and declared the playground open.

'Beats being in the numeracy hour!' Gurdip whispered to Tricia.

Tricia laughed, and said, 'But Miss Fardon will think of some maths we can do about the playground. You wait and see.'

✦ Conclusion

If our lives are to get better, and our surroundings are to improve, then we can't just sit back. We have to speak up about what we want. Adults can vote in elections. People have to be willing to do things as well as just complain about things. As the story shows us, children have opinions to offer about the things that affect them, and in the years to come they will be listened to more and more.

☀ A prayer

Lord, we thank you for the gift of play and being able to enjoy each other's company in games and activities. And we thank you, too, for moments of quiet and being able just to sit and think or talk quietly. Help us all to realise that we need to do both. Amen.

☀ A thought

There is an old saying 'Pride goes before a fall', which means that if you think too much of yourself, and don't listen to others, then you will make a mistake.

Song suggestions

'One more step', *Come and Praise*, 47

'The building song', *Alleluya*, 59

Day and night

Assembly 1 of 4

This assembly draws the attention of young children to the rhythm of the day: morning, afternoon, evening and night. Using a story based on a Central European myth, it shows that each has its place and is to be welcomed as it arrives.

You will need

• nothing at all.

Taken by ....

Date ....

Given to ....

Comments

● ....

● ....

● ....

✦ Introduction

If you always have a 'good morning everyone' routine, start from that. If not, just start here.

Good morning!

We always start the day like that don't we? We always say 'Good morning'.

And when we go to bed at night what do we say?

Good night!

What other times of the day do we use like that? Who can tell me?

There's 'Good afternoon', 'Good evening', or we might even say 'Good day', because that covers all of the other times together.

We never say 'Bad morning' do we? Even when it's raining, and we're feeling very miserable. We never put on a long face and say *(adopt an appropriate expression here)* 'Bad morning everybody!' or 'Really horrible morning everybody'.

No. Even if it's raining, and we're all wet and miserable, and everything has gone wrong, we still smile and say 'Good morning everybody'.

That's because what we are saying isn't really what we are thinking about the morning at all.

What we are saying is that we wish all our friends to have a good morning. If I say 'Good morning' to you, I am saying 'I really hope that you have a good morning'. And we can say that even if the weather is bad. We can wish that all the people around us will have a really good morning, full of good things.

Let's remember that and say 'Good morning everybody' again.

Now let's think about four times of the day:
morning
afternoon
evening
night.

Let's find four people to come out and be morning, afternoon, evening and night.

(Four volunteers out to the front.)

Day and night

Who will be morning?

This is morning, filled with cheerfulness and hope.

Optional

(*If the weather's not good.*) The weather's not so good this morning, so let's cheer ourselves up. It's still the start of a new day.

Dancing around, bright and lively!

Encourage the volunteer to do it.

The morning gradually goes away – there she goes, slowing down and moving to the side. And who comes along now?

This is the afternoon. A bit more serious after a day of hard work. Sitting at a desk working hard. Plenty of things done since the morning went away.

Again, encourage the mime.

Then she looks around, puts her work away, stands up and moves away, because the afternoon is coming to an end. And who is this coming along to take her place?

This is the evening. The evening is warm and comfortable. The evening is at home, having tea with the family, feeling comfortable and telling of all the things that have happened during the day.

Mime again.

The evening stands up and stretches and yawns. She is very tired. The daylight is fading, and it is time for her to move away and for night to come along.

This is the night.

The night is dark and quiet, like velvet. The night lies sleeping, safe and sound. The stars and the moon keep watch (*mime again*). And night sleeps safely until the morning comes

again. Look, here comes the morning, tiptoeing along, ready to take over all bright and lively (*mime*).

You can run this through again, now that the pupils know what to do. Use this rhyming commentary:

Here's the brand new morning, dancing on his way

Wide awake and full of strength, he starts our working day.

Along now comes the afternoon, to take the morning's place

Afternoon has done so much, he moves at a slower pace.

The evening's here now, safe at home, talking of all she's done

Of work in class and play with friends – some tears, but lots of fun.

The evening yawns and stretches, and she steals off out of sight

And now we see, all warm in sleep, the dark and gentle night.

Soon daylight comes, and seeks for night, to chase her right away

The morning's here, awake again, to bring another day.

Now here's a story.

📖 **Reading**

On a distant mountain top, the morning stood tall, his robes glowing with the gold of dawn. Above him, the dark sky was filled with a million stars. 'Time to go, you stars!' he called, his voice echoing through the mountains and into the purple heavens. Then he bent and picked up a huge rock. He bent his mighty arm

Day and night

and flung the rock high into the air, so that it plunged into the night sky, scattering the stars in all directions. 'Off you go, you stars. My time has come.'

Morning flung his arms high and wide. His golden robe billowed in the morning breeze, and the dark sky became light, first with the golden glow of dawn, and then blue as the sun emerged from behind morning's golden robe and filled the whole earth with the brightness of the sun.

On the mountain top, Morning danced his dawn dance, golden hair flying and golden robe spreading out on each side as he twisted and turned.

On and on went Morning's dance, across the mountains and down on to the plains, crossing rivers and chasing through villages and towns. Below, the lights in the towns went out, and the people stretched and started to get out of bed and go about their daily work.

Then, his energy nearly spent he slowed down to a walk. 'My I am tired.'

'I should think so!' said a familiar voice.

'Oh it's you again!' said Morning. Standing nearby was a beautiful figure dressed from head to foot in green. 'It's Afternoon. Here already?'

'Time for you to go, Morning! Time for me to take over!'

And Morning, his robes fading and his golden brightness becoming dim retreated slowly to his mountain top, where he sank down out of sight.

Afternoon went on his way at an altogether more dignified pace, basking in the peace of the day, listening to the sound of the birds and stopping to look at the flowers by the roadside.

'The trouble with Morning,' he thought, 'is that just to look at him makes you feel it's time to slow down. All that dancing! And all that rushing about! And all that glowing and shining! My! I'm for something with a bit more dignity and a bit of time to think.'

As Afternoon went on, at a steady pace, through the fields and the towns and villages, the light in the sky grew more mellow. People began to return to their homes as their daily work ended. Then, as he came to some trees, he spotted a familiar figure dressed in rich robes of orange and red. 'It's Evening. Is it your turn now?'

Evening spoke slowly and in a very relaxed tone of voice. 'Oh yes!' she said. 'Off you go now. Here I am to finish off the day.'

She stretched herself and slowly arose, and moved steadily and in a very stately way across the fields and through the villages and the towns. All around her the light grew red as the sun dipped down. The shadows lengthened, and the moon appeared in the darkening sky. One by one a star or two, brighter and bolder than the others, came back to the places where Morning, hours before, had chased them. In the towns and villages, people sat to eat their evening meals and to talk of the events of the day.

Evening strode on, at ease with herself, at peace and conscious of the shortness of her task. For soon it would be time to hand over. And sure enough, round a bend she came across the splendid figure of Night.

Night was tall and wonderful, dressed in billowing robes of deepest purple, with specks of silver and gold that seemed to wink on and off as the robe moved in the breeze. The robes came right up around Night's head, and you had to look hard to see her eyes, sharp and

Day and night

bright, among the folds. 'Welcome, Evening!' she said in her gentle but firm voice. 'Time for you to hand over to me now!'

Evening gratefully gave up her task, and returned, her orange glory fading, to her resting place.

Night turned to the west, spread her wonderful purple cloak with the sparkling points of light, and raced silently, but at great speed, across the land, as darkness spread across the sky and the stars and the moon shone ever brighter. Below, lights came on in the towns and villages, as people saw Night arrive and pass by on her way. Soon, they would be off to bed, soothed by the darkness and sure that Morning would soon be here again.

On and on she sped, across continents and seas until in the far distance, she spied just a speck of golden light. 'There's Morning again!' she said. 'We've done our job well, and it will soon be time to start again!'

✦ Conclusion

People have always been thankful for the rhythm of day and night – for the newness of morning, the brightness of the day, the comforting peace of evening and the mysterious darkness of the night.

Which is your favourite? Put up your hand.
Is it morning?
Or afternoon?
Or evening?
Or night time?

Whichever it is, you can be certain that they are all important. If there were no morning, the night would not end. If there were no afternoon, we would have no time for work or play. If there were no evening, we would miss

a precious time with families and friends. And if there were no night we would have no time for rest and quiet and sleep.

As each new morning comes, we have the chance to start again. We can leave yesterday's mistakes and tears behind. It will be better today!

Morning, afternoon, evening and night are all equally important, all part of the never ending rhythm that marks out our lives. We must make the most of each of them, and enjoy the differences between them.

☀ A prayer

Dear God, we thank you for the golden morning, bright afternoon, quiet evening and peaceful night. You made them for our health and comfort. Help us to enjoy them to the full, and to welcome each one as it arrives. Amen.

☀ A thought

Life would be unbearable if nothing ever changed. If the sun shone all the time we would soon grow tired of it. If it were dark all the time we would long for morning. We thrive on change. We should welcome change and not be upset by it.

Song suggestions

'Morning has broken', *Come and Praise*, 1

'Father we thank you for the night', *Someone's Singing Lord*, 1

Stepping out

Assembly 2 of 4

This assembly for the start of a new year or school year is particularly useful for a junior school that has taken pupils on from the infants. It uses the imagery of treading on unbroken snow.

You will need

• a list of new pupils' names.

Taken by ....

Date ....

Given to ....

Comments

⬤ ....

⬤ ....

⬤ ....

✦ Introduction

Today, we're going to think about beginnings. It's fairly obvious why we might do this at the start of a *new year/new school year/new school session/new term*.

Some of you are here for the first time and we will be thinking especially of you. But it's a beginning for all of us.

There are new people to meet, new classes to go to and a whole new school year to look forward to.

It's September now and, as our school year begins, we start thinking of autumn.

After autumn, we will start thinking of winter. In winter, we think of snow.

Let's try and think forward in time for a moment.

Can you remember what a snowy morning looks like?

When you wake up on a snowy morning there's something different, but you can't really tell what it is at first.

Then you realise that the light is somehow brighter on the ceiling, you look out of the window and the world has turned white overnight!

Imagine living in a house far out in the countryside.

Imagine looking out of your front door on a morning when it has snowed in the night.

Imagine a pure white blanket on the ground, stretching as far as you can see across the fields and hills, crisp and gleaming in the morning sunlight.

Then imagine pulling on your wellingtons or boots and putting on your coat, gloves and scarf and stepping out into the snow.

You are the first person to set foot in the new snow.

You make footprints away from your house and you look back to see them.

Stepping out

Then you turn again, to the pure white and unbroken snow, and you continue making footprints in it.

On and on you go across the silent, white fields.

From time to time, you look back to see where you have come from and you see your footprints leading from your home.

Then you turn forward again and go on making marks in the brand new snow.

Can you imagine what that would feel like?

Not many people have done it, but it isn't difficult to imagine what a good feeling it would be.

I can also imagine that you might be thinking, 'What's snow got to do with the beginning of a new school year?' Well, quite a lot actually.

In September, the days stretch ahead. Through the autumn term to Christmas and then through the spring to Easter. Then again from Easter through the summer term to the next summer holidays.

From here, it looks like unbroken white snow, waiting for us to cross and leave our footprints.

All of us will cross it together, each leaving a different set of footprints.

When we look back, we will see clearly where we have come from and how much progress we have made.

A lot of you have trodden the snow before with me. You have been in this assembly before at the beginning of a school year.

For some of you it is your last school year, and when you reach the end of the fields here, there will be new pastures waiting ahead.

Some of you are joining us on this journey for the very first time. Be brave and we will take you with us. Your footprints will be next to ours, just as important and just as confident.

So we welcome all of you this September morning. We welcome all our old friends and we welcome our new ones.

✦ Activity

I have a list of our new pupils here and I'll read them out one by one.

As I read out the name of each new pupil, I'd like him or her to stand up.

They could put up a hand if you think they would be more comfortable with that.

I will say, 'We welcome you to our school.'

Go through the names doing this. Give each pupil a big smile as you do so.

✦ Conclusion

Today, we are starting on our journey.

Are you ready to join us on this journey through the coming year?

We don't know exactly what sort of journey it will be – there will be good times and there will be difficult times.

But together we will make it an exciting and enjoyable time – a time to remember.

Stepping out

☀ A prayer

Dear God, be with all of us assembled here at the start of a new school year. Help us as we step out together.

May we have a good year, with new friends, new things to do and real progress.

Help our new pupils to settle in and remind us always to bear their needs in mind. Amen.

☀ A thought

Everybody was new once. Everybody had a first day at school.

We can help to make sure that the people who are starting today will look back on their first day with happiness.

Song suggestions

'Butterflies in my tummy', *Primary Assembly Song Book*, 22

'The building song', *Come and Praise*, 61

Optional follow up

- Extend the footprints symbolism in a display marking achievements and times of reflection or develop it in a drama activity.

- Talk about what the children hope to achieve in the coming year and what they feel they gained from the previous year.

Why giraffes have long necks

Why giraffes have long necks • OHT

Why giraffes have long necks

Assembly 3 of 4

This assembly is about evolution. It explains evolution through natural selection by means of a conversation between an adult and some children at the zoo.

You will need

• the OHT provided.

Taken by ....

Date ....

Given to ....

Comments

⚬ ....

⚬ ....

⚬ ....

✦ Introduction

There are many stories of how the world and its creatures came into being and because of the work of scientists and archaeologists we have learned more about how animals, plants and humans are the way they are now. This assembly tries to explain why one creature is quite different from others.

Have you been to a zoo? A trip to the zoo with a friend or relative is a good way of spending a summer afternoon.

Here are Tim and Nat at the zoo with their Aunt Phil. While they are there, they come up against one of the great truths of creation.

📖 Story

Put up the OHT provided.

'Well,' said Tim. 'There's no mistaking this one. It's a giraffe!'

'How could you tell?' asked Nat, rather sarcastically. 'Apart from its long neck that is.'

'Aunt Phil,' asked Tim. 'Why does it have such a long neck? It's supposed to eat the trees, but look at that one now, he's bending down to the grass and he has to spread his front legs to get his head down.'

Aunt Phil nodded. 'In the wild, he grazes on the leaves of trees and he needs the height. If he couldn't get down to ground level at all that would be a problem, but as you can see, he does it quite easily.'

'How does he come to have such a long neck?' asked Nat.

'That's a long story,' said Aunt Phil. 'It's all to do with evolution and with natural selection.'

'I know about that,' said Tim. 'It means that as time went on, giraffes' necks got longer and longer, so they could reach higher trees.'

'Yes, up to a point,' said Aunt Phil. 'Evolution does mean that living things gradually change to suit their surroundings.'

'I see,' said Nat. 'Giraffes stretched up and stretched their necks, and that meant their babies were born with longer necks.'

Why giraffes have long necks

Aunt Phil shook her head.

'It sounds logical, but it's not that,' she said. 'You see that might mean that if a dog learned to hop on a chair and then onto the table to get to food, then its puppies would be born able to do the same, which is just not so. If an animal learns something, or changes a habit or its appearance during its life, it's called an "acquired characteristic". Some scientists used to think that acquired characteristics could be passed on and that was how evolution happened. We are now sure that it's not like that.'

'So what is it like?' asked Nat.

'Hmm,' said Aunt Phil. 'Suppose giraffes all originally had short necks. Then, quite by accident, one was born with a longer neck. It would be able to eat the trees, so it would be stronger and more able to survive. Its babies would have longer necks too and they would be more able to survive. Then, many years later, perhaps quite by accident, one would be born with a longer neck still and be even more able to survive. And so on.'

Nat and Tim nodded slowly.

Aunt Phil waved her hands about as she said, 'That's very simplified, but that's what it is. Every newborn creature is a little different from its parents. Just occasionally, one of these changes is a help to its survival.

'It lives on when others die – perhaps it can see better, or reach its food better, or swim more strongly, or find its way back to its nest better. That change is handed on, and those animals with the change survive while others do not. Those most suited to their surroundings survive best and they hand on to their descendants the characteristics that make them able to survive.'

'And so?' asked Nat.

'And so,' said Aunt Phil, 'we have giraffes with long necks, cats with retractable claws, hawks that can hover perfectly still in the air, bats that find flying insects by bouncing echoes from them – all the astonishing wonders of nature in fact, including, I might say, yourselves.'

'It's amazing!' said Tim.

'It's more than that,' said Aunt Phil. 'It's a miracle!'

✦ Conclusion

Everything to do with creation and the development of the universe, the Earth and its living inhabitants is difficult to understand – a real challenge to the imagination.

Evolution – the gradual adaptation of living things so they can deal with their surroundings – is wonderful and beautiful.

It has happened over such an incredibly long time that we cannot really imagine it. All of the history of human beings is just a tiny part of the history of life on this planet.

It's hard to find words to describe such awesome ideas, so let's be quiet and think of the living world around us. Think of its richness and variety, of the beauty of all living things and the astonishing ways they have of coping with their surroundings.

I'll remind you of some of the great wonders of the natural world. After each one, take a moment of silence to reflect on just how amazing it is.

Optional

You can make this into a prayer by replacing 'Think of' with 'We thank you Lord for'.

Why giraffes have long necks

Think of the miraculous ability of bats to navigate in the dark using echoes.

Think of plants that have found ways of eating insects.

Think of pet dogs that walk in a circle before they lie down, because their ancestors have passed on a dog's instinct to clear a space in the grass.

Think of birds that have the skill to build elaborate nests.

Think of salmon that find their way across the oceans, and up rivers, to breed.

Let's just be silent for a moment and be in awe of all of that.

The science of evolution is difficult to understand and difficult to explain. Sometimes, all we can do is try to put our thoughts into a song, a poem or a piece of drama.

A prayer

Dear God, we stand in awe and wonder at the living world around us, which we still do not begin to understand completely.

We thank you for its richness and variety, and for the way that it has developed over many millions of years.

Help us always to respect living things of all kinds, so that they can continue to develop over the millions of years still to come. Amen.

A thought

All around us there is change – we grow, the seasons change, the weather changes, each day is different from the last. We should see those changes as new starts and ways to improve our lives and the lives of those around us.

Song suggestions

'God who made the Earth', *Come and Praise*, 10

'Everything', *Primary Assembly Song Book*, 4

Optional follow up

Continue the topic of evolution and natural selection in class. Talk about Darwin and the scientific approach to creation.

Time capsule

Assembly 4 of 4

This assembly is about the placing of a time capsule in the foundations of a new school building. It is a turning point for the school and for the people involved.

You will need

- nothing at all.

Taken by ....

Date ....

Given to ....

Comments

⬤ ....

⬤ ....

⬤ ....

✦ Introduction

In our assembly today we look at ways in which we can preserve our memories of our lives today so that future generations can look back and see what life was like in our time. We can also look forward to the changes we can expect to happen in our lifetime.

• • • • • • • • • • • •

I know of somebody who was taking up the floorboards in his house to put in some central heating pipes. It was a very old house, and the floorboards had never been up before.

Under the floorboards, apart from a lot of dust and a mouse's nest, he found a collection of newspapers tied up with string. They were very old newspapers – all of them for the year 1926.

Now the year 1926 was an eventful one – there was a General Strike, when workers in all the mines and the railways and lots of other industries stopped working for a while. It was an important political event.

Whoever put those newspapers there probably didn't do it by accident. They wanted someone in the future to know something about the time they lived in.

It's not at all unusual for people to do that – to put newspapers under the floorboards, or to write on the wall before they put wallpaper on.

If you do the job in an organised way – get a proper container and choose things to put in, and then bury the container – then it's called making a time capsule.

It may never be found, but you hope it will be found a hundred or more years in the future. You choose things for a time capsule that will help people to understand what your life was like, and the times you lived in.

It's interesting to think about what you might put in a time capsule – and perhaps you could do that in class.

In our story today, Teresa and Sean and Michael, and their father Danny, all attend a time capsule ceremony.

Time capsule

📖 **Story**

Teresa and Sean and Michael all brought the same letter home – which was very unusual because they were in different schools.

'Dear Parents,' it said.

'Next Thursday, the 21st, we will be laying the foundation stone of our brand new sports hall.

'As you know, the sports hall will be available for the schools on the site, and also for the local community. For that reason the schools will be involved, as well as our neighbours from the community.

'We hope you can be there at three o'clock. Everyone is welcome.'

The letter didn't finish there. It went on.

'An important part of the ceremony will be the placing of a time capsule under the foundation stone.

'Children from the schools have chosen items for the time capsule, and children will be involved in placing it.'

Danny, the children's dad, read all three letters, just to be fair, even though they were exactly the same.

'Are you coming, Dad?' asked Michael. 'I've got to do something at the ceremony.'

Sean and Teresa looked at him. 'Really?' asked Teresa. 'What are you doing to do? Tap dance?'

Michael shook his head quite seriously. 'No, I'm going to put something in the time capsule, and I have to read something out.'

'Well,' said Teresa. 'That's news to us. You'll have to come now, Dad.'

'That I will,' said Danny. 'I'll be there on the dot.'

The 21st was cold but sunny – a bright frosty day, early in the year, the kind of weather that made your breath visible and the ground hard – which was a good job, because it meant that people would not get their feet quite so muddy.

A crowd gradually gathered by the side of the building site that would, in a year or so, be the Alice Symons Memorial Sports Hall. In front of the site stood a wooden platform with a microphone, and behind the platform the foundation stone – about as big as a suitcase, but much heavier – was hanging in a cradle held by a mobile crane.

Danny walked across to join the crowd. The children from the schools had the best places at the front, and Danny looked to see if he could see his daughter and sons, but he couldn't spot them.

Then the headteachers and senior teachers of the schools stood up on the platform. Mrs Johnson, who was in charge of the infants, came forward to the microphone.

'I've been chosen to do this,' she said, 'because our children, the youngest ones, are a symbol of our hopes for the future. It's an honour for me to lay this foundation stone, and to remember Alice Symons, the councillor who worked so hard to make sure the sports hall would be built.

'Now,' she went on, 'we will place our time capsule under the stone, and the stone will be lowered into place. Before we do that, let me say a word about what is in the capsule – in

Time capsule

fact you all have a list of its contents in your programmes.' (Danny looked around for someone giving out programmes, but then had to share with the man standing next to him.)

'As you can see,' said Mrs Johnson, 'the children from the schools have chosen things that they think represent the time in which we live – there's a computer game, a *TV Times*, a brochure for the new Jaguar, a Harry Potter book and so on. All of them imaginative.

'But there was one, chosen by a boy in my school, that I thought was more thoughtful and imaginative than any of the others. I asked him to write down the reasons why he had chosen this item, and what he wrote interested me, and I think it will interest you. So I want Michael Sullivan to come up here and read to you what he wrote.'

Danny craned his neck to see, and there was Michael climbing up to the platform. Danny shushed the people near him and tilted his head to listen. Michael spoke into the microphone.

'When I came here, I was unhappy at first,' he read. 'I missed my friends and my old home. I missed being able to see hills from the window of the school and I missed being near the sea.

'But my teachers and the other children were kind to me and I made new friends, and I belong here now.

'What I have chosen for the time capsule is a special book that my teacher at my old school gave me when I left. It has photographs of my school, and the village where we lived, and cuttings from the newspaper for the time I was living there. There were some troubles in my village, with bombs and guns, and they are in the newspaper cuttings.

'My teacher wrote in it for me, wishing me luck. She asked me to take care of it. I think that if I put it in the time capsule I am taking care of it. I also think that if it is there it will be safe, and I will be able to stop thinking about it all the time.

'That time is in my mind, but it is better now for me to think about my new friends and my new home.'

Michael stopped and everyone was silent for a moment. They were all wondering whether it was right to put something like that under the ground in a time capsule.

Danny wondered, too. He knew that scrapbook and he knew that Michael spent a lot of time looking at it. At the same time he understood what Michael was doing. He was finding a way of leaving his old life behind, and yet not forgetting it altogether. The book would be safe in the time capsule. One day somebody would find it, and the memories would come alive again for them.

Gradually, applause started and spread until everyone was clapping Michael. Danny nodded and spoke under his breath to himself. 'Good boy, Michael. Good boy.'

At the front, Michael helped the heads and the foreman from the site to lower the capsule into a special space under the foundation stone. Then the foundation stone came down on top of it.

The mayor stepped forward and tapped the foundation stone with a wooden mallet and made his own brief speech.

Time capsule

'Young Michael has it right,' he said. 'This is a time for putting the past in its rightful place and looking to a new future. I will say no more. I declare this foundation stone well and truly laid.' And he tapped the stone with his wooden mallet and everyone clapped again.

Danny looked around again while the clapping was going on, and tried hard to see Sean and Teresa. Eventually he spotted Sean, who was laughing with his friends – one of the teachers was frowning at him.

Then he saw Teresa, also with a group of friends. Teresa saw him looking and she raised her eyebrows and gestured towards Michael. Danny put his thumb up, and she laughed.

As the crowd dispersed, Danny smiled to himself. It had been a difficult six months, but things were not going so badly now. Still problems to come, he thought, but that's to be expected with young people.

✦ Conclusion

The three children and their father came from a troubled part of the world. They had good friends there, and lots of happiness, but Danny wanted to put difficult memories behind and bring his children to a more peaceful place. They didn't find it easy at first, but things were settling down now.

Michael, in his own way, buried the past – but in a way which kept it safely locked away.

What Michael did was very difficult in some ways. He had something that he treasured – a book from his old teacher, made specially for him. It couldn't have been easy for him to give it up. And yet in giving it up he was showing how much it meant to him. He certainly wasn't throwing it away, or giving it away.

Whoever finds it, perhaps far into the future, will treasure it, too, and Michael and his story will be told again, perhaps in a newspaper. Michael has found a way of keeping his old life precious and yet putting it safely to one side so that he can get on with today and the future.

And that's probably about right. We should remember the past, because it's precious, but we should also keep our eyes fixed on the future.

☀ A prayer

Lord, help us to keep our precious memories of good times, but help us, too, to make the most of today and look forward and to prepare ourselves for the lives we have to come. Amen.

☀ A thought

In a corner of all our minds is a time capsule. Every now and again we visit it, and add something to it, then put it safely and carefully away again.

Song suggestions

'The best gift', *Come and Praise*, 59

'To build a memory', *Primary Assembly Song Book*, 49

Teams and competition

Assembly 1 of 4

This highlights teamwork and makes the point that competition depends on the friendly presence of a competitor. It is in two parts and you may want to use it for two consecutive assemblies.

You will need

• a blank OHT and pens.

Taken by ....

Date ....

Given to ....

Comments

● ....

● ....

✦ Introduction

We're celebrating achievements today. Especially the achievements of our school teams. We're proud of our teams, because of the way they enjoy their games and because they give us something to enjoy too – lots of us like jumping up and down and shouting to cheer them on! And, of course, whether they win or lose they know that they bring credit to the school. *(Add something about the particular team you are celebrating.)*

Now let me tell you about when Charles Street School Netball Team was in the final of the town cup.

📖 Story 1

The Charles Street School Netball team were having a good year. They had won every game in the knockout competition. They had even beaten St Barnabas in the semi final, and St Barnabas had won the cup for three years running.

Now it was the final, and they were up against Martindale Junior. They were looking forward to playing them. Martindale was a good team, and it was going to be a great match.

On the morning of the match all the team went on the school minibus to Stockwell Road School, because the final was always played on a neutral pitch. The minibus was followed by a whole parade of cars full of people who were going to support them.

But the match didn't happen. The Martindale Team didn't turn up. All sorts of things went wrong for Martindale.

Mrs Roberts, the games teacher, had got up especially early as she had to drive from her house to the local secondary school to pick up the minibus. Martindale didn't have their own bus, so they were borrowing the secondary school's.

First she had a problem at home – her car wouldn't start and she had to fix it first. Then when she got to the secondary school the gates were locked and she had to go and find the caretaker in his house. That made her later still. By then she was frantic.

At Martindale, the team were waiting with the school helper. They didn't know what to do. There weren't any other cars to go in – their parents and the other teachers had said that they would meet them at Stockwell Road. So they all waited.

Teams and competition

Meanwhile, Mrs Roberts had finally managed to get the minibus out of the secondary school. Then as she was driving along, it spluttered and came to a stop. It had run out of diesel!

Mrs Roberts had to walk to the garage and get a can of diesel. She tried to ring Martindale from the garage, but nobody answered because there was nobody in the office of course.

Mr Wilkinson, the head of Martindale, was at the pitch. He was getting really worried. The time for the start of the match came and went, and he wondered if the minibus had been in an accident. He was very anxious indeed!

He got in his car and drove to Martindale. He was relieved to find the team still standing there with the school helper. He could have got some of the team in his car, but it wasn't big enough for everyone. They decided they just had to wait for the minibus. In any case he was really worried about what had happened and he wanted to find out.

Meanwhile back at Stockwell, the teachers had decided that they just had to call the match off. They couldn't wait for ever, because parents were expecting their children home, and lots of people had other things to do later in the day.

The head of Stockwell Road, Mrs Armitage, was Chair of the Sports Association, and she called a quick meeting of the teachers. She asked whether she should award the cup to Charles Street because they had turned up and Martindale hadn't.

But Mr Gilbert, the head of Charles Street, was quite sure that they shouldn't win the cup without playing. He explained it to the children, 'We want to win, but we can't win when we haven't beaten anybody! It's only fair that Martindale are allowed to play in the final – they've been working as hard for it as we have. We all think that we should arrange to have the match again in a couple of weeks. I hope you all agree.'

There were a few murmurs and mumbles between the girls – they had been really looking forward to today, and they were a bit disappointed that they hadn't been able to play. But no one disagreed – it would feel a bit funny showing everyone their winners medals and then telling them that they hadn't actually played. It wouldn't really feel like winning.

Two weeks later, the match happened, and nothing went wrong. Martindale and Charles Street played a good, very closely fought game. Who won? To be honest, I can't quite remember, because it was a long time ago.

What everyone does remember about that match was the way that everyone got on and sorted out the problems together. The teachers from the three schools that were involved got together and came to a decision to hold the match on another day.

The girls in the teams went back to their schools and practised hard so that they would be even better for the new match, and all the supporters agreed to turn out again on the new date to do their jumping and cheering.

No one grumbled that the original game hadn't gone as planned. No one made Mrs Roberts feel like it was her fault for being late.

Everyone – the teachers, the players, the helpers and the supporters – worked together as a real team to make the new day as exciting an occasion as they could.

✦ Commentary

We are always having to work as teams. We teachers work as a team, and you all often work in teams in the classroom and when you play sports.

Teams and competition

There are lots of times when it's important that we work together, get on with each other, and encourage each other.

Even in competitions your competitors are your friends, because you measure yourself against them. If they are good, you must try to be better. If you are good they will try harder to match up to you.

Now, can some of you tell me what your favourite team sports are? What do you like to watch on TV? *Take suggestions. If someone mentions motor racing, say 'Well done! Somebody mentioned motor racing.' Or if they don't, say 'So nobody thought of motor racing.'*

I like to watch motor racing. Does anybody else? One of my favourite drivers is Nigel Mansell. He was Formula One World Champion in 1992, then in 1993 he was Indycar Champion in the USA. You might not think of him as being part of a team. When he's actually racing, he's on his own isn't he? But let me tell you a true story about how important being part of a team is to him.

📖 Story 2

It was a big race and Nigel Mansell was in the lead. His Williams car was better than the others, it had a fast Renault engine and it had computers controlling the suspension so that it could corner faster than the other cars. As he drove, he talked to Frank Williams, the Williams team leader, on the radio.

Frank said, 'Nigel, how does the car feel, over?'

Nigel replied, 'Frank, it's fine, the oil pressure is good, the suspension is good, just fine, over.'

'Good, you're 30 seconds in the lead now so don't push it, take it easier, over,' said Frank.

'Thirty seconds, great, what do you think about the tyres, over?' asked Nigel.

'Well, it's best not to take any chances, if you call in at the pits next lap round we'll fit new ones, over,' said Frank.

'OK, we don't want any punctures, over and out,' said Nigel.

The pits are the place where the cars go to have quick repairs and quick tyre changes done. If a car needs to go to the pits the race carries on and the problem then is that the other cars catch up.

But Nigel wasn't worried, he had a 30-second lead and it usually only took 12 seconds to get tyres changed. He could be in and out and still be ahead of the other cars.

In the pits the team of mechanics were getting ready. They had got the new tyres out and had put electric warmers around them to warm them up. Now they were ready and waiting. There was one mechanic holding each tyre. Another was in charge of an electric nut spanner, his job was to loosen the old wheel and tighten up the new one. There was also a mechanic in front with STOP and GO signs.

Of course they couldn't take the wheels off when the car was on the ground, so they needed one more mechanic. He looked after the front end jack and the rear end jack which lifted the car up.

Each of them had to do their job quickly – they only had 12 seconds. They'd practised for many hours, racing against the stop-watch.

Nigel Mansell drove his car into the pits. The STOP sign shot up and the car screeched to a halt.

The front jack went into action and the rear jack lifted up too.

The drills started up, spinning off the wheel nuts. The old wheels came off. The new wheels were attached as quickly as possible, with the

Teams and competition

drills whirring once again. As soon as each wheel was on, a hand went up. Once all four wheels were attached, the jacks came down and the STOP sign dropped.

Then the GO sign shot up. 'Go Nigel, go!' shouted the crowd.

The car set off, the wheels spinning as it left the pit. But something was wrong! Everybody stared. At the rear of the car, one wheel was not fixed and it spun off in a great arc.

The car, which was still in the lead, suddenly shuddered to a grinding halt, its suspension was ruined as it slid along the tarmac. Nigel Mansell could only sit and watch as first the Hondas then the Ferraris and soon all the other cars shot past.

Meanwhile in the pits, there was no talking, one mechanic knew which wheel it was that had come off. It was the rear driver's side wheel, his wheel, his job to tighten it up.

✦ Follow up

Next day, when the Williams team were back at headquarters, they had a meeting to talk about what went wrong. I'm going to write two things on the OHP, and I want you to decide which of the two things the team managers did at their meeting.

1 Told off the mechanic for not doing his job properly.

2 Worked out what to do to make things better next time.

Who thinks it was 1? Who thinks it was 2? Who thinks it was both?

Well, it was 2. Think about it. There was no point in telling the mechanic off. He knew he had got it wrong. The important thing was to make sure that it didn't happen again.

The team leader knew that it was better to work out how to put it right. than to waste time telling off good team members who were doing their best.

When a driver wins a race it is him who goes up on to the podium and shakes the huge bottle of champagne. Down below, the pits team watch and know that they were in the team. The driver didn't do it on his own

☀ A prayer

Dear God, help us to enjoy sport and, when we have the chance, help us to enjoy taking part in sport. If somebody in our team isn't doing very well, if they have a bad time, help us to encourage them with words that support them and not to moan at them and make things worse. In turn, when we make mistakes bless us with kind words around us, which build us up to do better. Amen.

☀ A thought

Competition is not unfriendly. We need our competitors if we are to do well. Without our competitors the game does not exist. We also need our team members. They want to do well. When they make a mistake, we all take a share of the responsibility, for that is what teamwork is.

Song suggestions

'Make me a channel of your peace', *Alleluya*, 43

'The family of man', *Come and Praise*, 69

The Boat Race

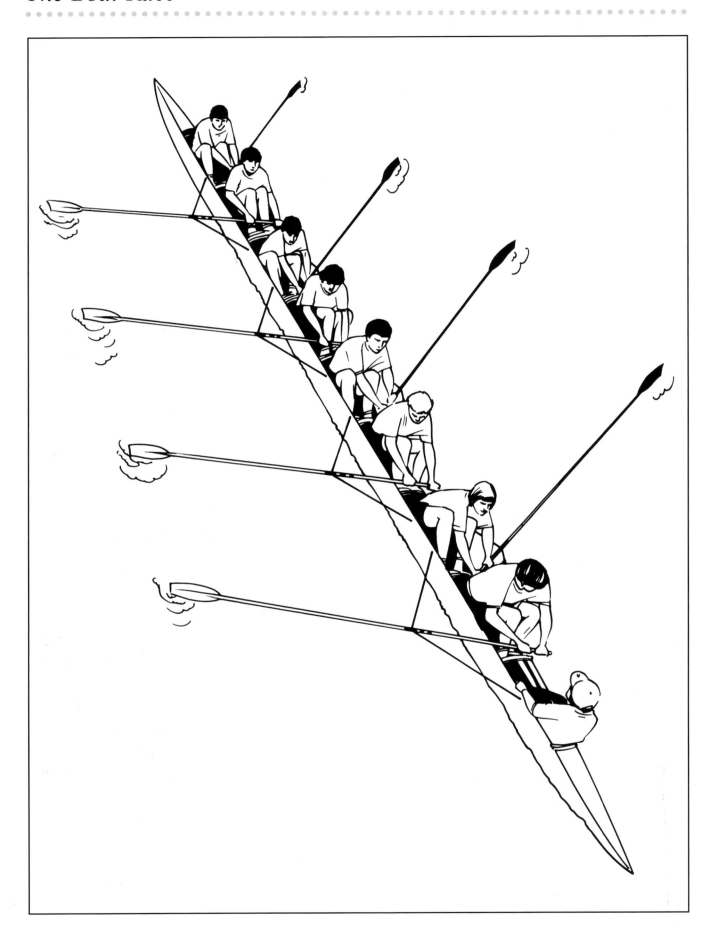

The Boat Race

Assembly 2 of 4

This assembly is intended for the week leading up to the Oxford v Cambridge Boat Race. It provides some background facts about rowing and emphasises the importance of teamwork.

You will need

• the OHT provided.

Taken by	....	....	....
Date	....	....	....
Given to	....	....	....

Comments

⬤ ....

⬤ ....

✦ Introduction

There is a very famous race that takes place on the River Thames in London between Oxford University and Cambridge University.

It is called the Boat Race and they row from Putney to Mortlake and their rowing, or racing, boats look like this.

Put up the OHT provided.

You can see that there are nine people in this boat – eight people to row and one person to steer.

Each rower has one oar, so there are four oars on each side of the boat.

The person who steers sits at the back and is called the cox. The cox needs to be small and light so that they don't make the boat too heavy and so the rowers can go as fast as possible.

These rowers are all men, but there are races for women too. There are races for single rowers and for various numbers up to eight.

Do you think that the boat can go very fast?

Well it goes faster than most of us can run. It would take a good athlete to keep up with the boat race running on the bank. During practise, the coach often rides a bike along the bank to keep up.

✦ Activity

Now let's try to put together our own team. Who will be the cox?

Position the volunteer at the front.

Now, who will be the eight rowers?

Position these volunteers in a line facing the cox.

Now you're ready to get into your boat. It's a very tricky job, because the boat is very narrow. It's narrow so that it has good speed through the water.

The boat is beautifully made from wood or from a more expensive material, such as carbon fibre, and is designed to slip easily through the water. But it's not easy to get into it without tipping it up.

The cox gets in first. Here you go. Steady!

Then the others. Very carefully…

I'll hand them their oars and push them out into the river.

The Boat Race

Now, start rowing.

Chaos will probably follow.

Stop!

What's wrong? *(Take suggestions if appropriate.)*

They're not rowing together.

They need to row in time. How will they do that?

First, let's see what the action of rowing is. We can all do that together.

Demonstrate the following actions as you are saying them.

Hold the oar in front of you with two hands.

Lean forward with your arms straight out, level with the top of your stomach.

Now lift your arms just a little so that the blade of the oar drops into the water, and lean back, pulling the oar back to push the boat forward. Keep your arms straight.

When you've leaned well back, finish the stroke by bending your arms to pull the oar into your body.

In a boat with two, four or eight people, all the rowers need to work together.

Hold on a moment! There is one other person working with the rowers – that person is the cox.

All the time, the cox is steering the boat and calling encouragement to the crew.

The cox has many crucial decisions to make which can win or lose the race. Is the boat clear of the rival boat? Which side of the river is best? Will the way the water is flowing make the boat go faster or slower? How will the weather affect the water?

Now, let's try our team again. Ready?

All together. Lean forward with your arms straight. Lift your arms to drop the oar into the water. Lean back to pull the oar. Bend your arms in.

And again. Lean forward with your arms straight. Lift your arms to drop the oar. Lean back to pull the oar. Bend your arms in.

Well done!

✦ Conclusion

Rowing might seem easy now on land, but it's not as easy on a flowing river with ripples on it.

It is tremendously athletic. Rowers are exceptionally strong, especially in the upper body and arms.

They also have excellent endurance. The Boat Race lasts about fifteen minutes. The rowers always say that after four minutes they feel totally exhausted. But there are another eleven minutes to go! They hang on and keep trying their best though.

Everyone in the boat depends on everyone else hanging on and doing their best. No one team member can let the others down. It is a very good example of teamwork.

When a team wins, it's not possible to say that one person did it.

In football, for example, you can pick out a good goal scorer, a goalkeeper or a penalty taker.

In a rowing eight, there are no stars. They're all team members.

So if you watch the boat race on Saturday, try to take notice of these things.

The Boat Race

- The work of the cox, steering and making crucial decisions.

- The huge effort, especially towards the end.

- The fact that you can't pick out stars.

- The rhythm and togetherness of each crew member.

- The total exhaustion at the end.

- The way the winning team celebrates together.

☀ A prayer

Dear God, we thank you for the enjoyment sport gives us and for the strength and teamwork it encourages.

Even if we don't think we are very good at a sport, we know we can have fun.

Remind us that everyone can join in and be a team member, because every team needs lots of different skills. Amen.

☀ A thought

Perhaps the best teams have no stars. Or if they do, perhaps the real stars are the ones who remember how much they need the support of other team members.

Teams like this aren't just in sport – they might be our class, our groups of friends, our families and the community we live in.

Song suggestions

'He who would valiant be', *Come and Praise*, 44

'The building song', *Alleluya*, 59

Optional follow up

- Video the boat race and show it, discussing the nature of the race.

- Talk about other sports where teamwork is important.

- Discuss how teamwork has helped the children achieve things already.

Working in harness

Assembly 3 of 4

This assembly deals with the problem of some
children who don't want to work together. The teacher
tells them a story about working in partnership and
using each other's strengths.

You will need

- nothing at all.

Taken by			
Date			
Given to			

Comments

● ....

● ....

● ....

✦ Introduction

It's not always easy to work with somebody
else. Sometimes you can't easily see why you
should do it, or what you can gain from it.

Mrs Fletcher's class were going through a bad
patch about this – children falling out, and not
wanting to work together.

'Come on, George,' Mrs Fletcher said one day,
'I really want you to work with Robert on this.
You'd be able to help each other.'

But George was in a sulk. 'Robert's too slow.
I don't like working with Robert,' he said.

Mrs Fletcher was annoyed. She didn't like
to hear her children being unkind to each
other. She decided to stop the work and tell
them a story.

'Right, on the carpet everybody. Time for a
story. This one is about two people who really
did cooperate with each other.'

📖 Story

Long ago, in Eastern Europe, there lived a
fourteen-year-old boy called Isaac. He lived
with his parents on a small farm a few miles
outside the town. They had a hard but happy
life, farming the land, looking after their
animals.

Isaac was unable to walk because of an
accident on the farm when he was very young.
His father had made him a wheelchair – there
were none to be had from the government in
that place – and he was a real help with such
jobs as milking the cows and feeding the
chickens.

Isaac was also a studious boy. He read a great
deal, and listened to a radio in his room and
he knew a great deal more about the world
than most of the people in his village. He was
a happy boy in many ways.

Then, one day, everything changed for the
family.

A squad of policemen came and told them that
they would have to leave their village, because
it was needed for other people.

Working in harness

'You cannot stay here, because you are Jewish people,' said the policeman. 'And we are removing all Jewish people from the villages in this area. You must go and live in a special area in the city.'

'But what about our animals and our land?' said Isaac's father. 'They are all the wealth that we have. We cannot earn a living without them. Farming is all that we know.'

'I can't help that,' said the chief policeman. 'By next week you, and all the others in the village who are like you, must be gone.'

* * * * * * * * * *

That night, the family talked long and hard about the future. Other families came to join them, and the Rabbi came too and together they tried to decide what to do.

'We may be able to manage in the city,' said the Rabbi. 'But the future is uncertain and I think our young people must be given the chance to leave to find a new life. Those who are old enough, and who want to leave, should go tomorrow on the train that stops here. After that it will be too late. The police will stop them.'

Isaac's father and mother looked at each other.

'Isaac cannot go,' said his father. 'You know that he needs to be cared for. The rest of you must make up your own minds with your own children.'

Isaac was deeply disappointed that he could not go with his friends, but he did not argue with his father. How could he manage in his wheelchair?

The next day, the dozen or so children and young people who were old enough to travel without their parents – some as young as eleven or twelve, looked after by older brothers and sisters – gathered at the station with their families.

The plan was that they would take local trains, avoiding the mainline expresses, which were watched by police, to the border at a little-used post in the deep countryside. Then on, hopefully to America or to England, where there were cousins and friendly communities.

Each young traveller had a name and an address safely in an inside pocket.

The young people stood by the door of the train. The grown-ups stood in a group watching.

Goodbyes had been said. Mothers had stroked the heads of the beloved sons and daughters who were about to disappear, perhaps for ever.

It was a heart-rending sight. Isaac was with his parents, in his home-made chair. Tears filled his eyes, for he was saying goodbye to friends he had spent his whole life with. It had all happened so quickly that no one had had time to think or prepare properly.

* * * * * * * * * *

Then, suddenly, there was a voice from among the young people gathered at the door of the train.

'Hey, why is Isaac not coming?'

It was Abe, one of Isaac's friends.

The Rabbi went to the group. 'You know why. He cannot manage this journey. He has to stay with his parents.'

'Nonsense!' said Abe. 'Let him come. I will look after him. I need him. Look at me. I am

Working in harness

strong and fit, but I do not have any of the brains and good sense that he has. I cannot even read. He can read anything. I need him.'

And with that Abe went to Isaac, looked at Isaac's mother and father and said, 'Let your son come with me. I will guard him with my life. Where I go he will go too. Where I end up, he will end up. Together we will overcome all difficulties. I promise you this, on my life.'

Isaac turned himself round to face his parents. 'Let me go, father. I need to be with my friends. I love you both, but I know that I have to do this.'

Isaac's father spread his arms in submission, and both tearful parents watched as Abe manhandled Isaac and his chair onto the train. Isaac hardly had time to speak, let alone say a proper goodbye.

As the train pulled out, Abe dragged Isaac upright to the window, and together they waved, two white faces at the misted window, disappearing to an uncertain future. The feelings of the adults left on the platform can easily be imagined.

• • • • • • • • • • • •

Abe worked like a madman on the journey, doing everything for the two of them. Sometimes he cradled Isaac like a baby in his arms and ran across a station footbridge. Then he would put him down by the wall and run back to carry the wheelchair. It was a superhuman effort, on a long and complicated rail and sea journey of fifteen hundred miles.

Isaac played his crucial part when there was talking to be done at borders and checkpoints, and when there were documents to be read and signed.

To the rough border guards, Isaac seemed to be a special kind of person – learned, fluent in speech, able to make sense of the papers that even the guards themselves could hardly read.

Isaac's confidence grew as he realised that he had a gift that was helping them both. 'I can do this,' he thought. 'Together we will make the journey to safety.'

• • • • • • • • • • • •

So it was that together they arrived in the East End of London, at the house of a distant cousin of Abe's father. The cousin was pleased to see Abe, but doubtful about Isaac.

'I'm not so sure we can look after him,' said the cousin. Abe snorted. 'He goes where I go. I go where he goes. If you send him to live in the street then you send me to live in the street. We are brothers now, he and I.'

So together they stayed, and in the end the cousin was glad that they had, for Abe and Isaac helped him with his business, which was making clothes for rich London customers.

The boys learned quickly – they learned to speak English and they learned the business. Abe's big-hearted personality and strength of character were real assets, and Isaac studied the workings of the office and eventually took over all of the book work and correspondence.

• • • • • • • • • • • •

Abe and Isaac grew to manhood, and gradually took over the clothing firm as the cousin grew older and eventually retired. Together they made it a huge and prosperous business, with many factories.

© **pfp** 2002 ISBN 1 874050 56 2 May be photocopied for use only within the purchasing institution **pfp**, 61 Gray's Inn Road, London WC1X 8TH

Working in harness

They grew rich, but they remained modest, always remembering their humble beginnings.

In the place of honour in their main offices was a painting they had commissioned, showing the scene on that station platform all those years before. And in the corner of their own private office was a home-made wheelchair.

People often asked about it, and Isaac was only too pleased to tell them.

'When we say that Abe and I are partners,' he would say, 'you think you know what that means. But let me tell you that you will never fully understand what partnership means to us. Through partnership, and through the unselfishness of our dear parents, we found life where there might have been only misery and death.'

✦ Conclusion

Mrs Fletcher finished the story. She looked at the class. She didn't really expect them to change in a moment, and suddenly become very kind to each other. But she knew things would gradually get better.

The children in the class had much to think about. They began to realise that the world they lived in had been shaped by people of great courage and talent. They realised that progress was often won by self-sacrifice, unselfishness and the ability to see the qualities of other people.

Mrs Fletcher could see that the class were starting to think about what she'd told them, and she decided that she'd think of other stories to tell, other visits to make. They'll get there in the end, she thought.

☀ A prayer

Lord, we thank you for our lives in school, for friendship, fellowship and the opportunity to work together on common problems and on the things we enjoy. Help us to overcome our differences and to be patient with each other. Amen.

☀ A thought

Come together to solve a problem and you may stay together to solve many problems.

Song suggestions

Same but different', *Primary Assembly Song Book*, 42

'One more step', *Come and Praise*, 47

Optional follow up

Research the recent history of the Jewish people in Russia and Europe – the pogroms, the Holocaust and persecutions since then.

In the science lab

Assembly 4 of 4

This assembly is about working together. It shows that people of widely differing age and experience can make good partnerships. The message is that working together can have effects beyond the work itself.

You will need

- nothing at all.

Taken by ....

Date ....

Given to ....

Comments

- ....
- ....
- ....

✦ Introduction

When you work together in class, or when you play together, do you just talk about the work or about the game? I don't think so.

One of the benefits of working with someone else is that you learn much more than you think you are going to. You learn something about the person you are working with, and that can help you to learn about yourself.

That's certainly what Mark finds in this story

📖 Story

Mark wasn't sure whether he was looking forward to the visit to the secondary school. His mum wasn't even sure why he was going.

'I could understand it if you were in Year 6,' she said, 'but you're only in Year 4. Why are you going there?'

'To do science,' he said, 'with one of the big ones. A sixth former, I think it is.'

'Well, we'll see,' said his mum.

When he got to Greendale Comp with the rest of the class, he still felt a bit frightened – it was such a big place, and even though there were lots of friendly people about, teachers and helpers, he rather wished he was back in his own familiar little school.

He was taken with the others to the science department – big benches, funny smells, people in white coats. A bit like a hospital really, he thought to himself, which didn't make him feel any less worried.

The Greendale teacher talked to them, but because Mark was a bit worried he didn't take much of it in. Then he found himself teamed up with a great big, tall girl.

She came across the room to him and said, 'Hi, Mark, I'm Daljit.' Mark grunted and shuffled his feet a bit.

'Come on then, Mark, we've got a bit of a project to do together,' she said.

She showed him to a place where there were two stools at one of the side benches in the lab. On the bench there was a workcard and some apparatus.

In the science lab

Mark sat up on one of the stools. Daljit sat up on the other.

'OK, Mark,' said Daljit. 'Read the card.'

Mark picked up the card. This was the moment he'd been dreading. This was why he hadn't really wanted to come. He looked at the card. The print was small. The words were long. The card was unfriendly looking, and a bit curled at the edges. He put the card down and bowed his head. Tears came.

Daljit was busy arranging the apparatus and she didn't notice at first. 'Come on, Mark,' she said, still not looking at him. 'Read the card so we know what we have to do.'

There was no reply. Daljit looked at Mark, but his head was down. She ducked her head to try to make contact. 'Mark?' she said. 'OK?'

Then she realised that Mark was crying. For a moment she didn't know what to do. Her first thought was to call the teacher over. She decided not to do that, though, because she knew it might well upset Mark even more. Somehow the two of them had to solve the problem together, whatever it was.

She put her hand on his shoulder. 'Come on, Mark, what is it? What's the matter?'

Mark looked up. 'I don't want to read the card,' he said. 'It's too hard.'

Daljit understood straightaway. She could have kicked herself. Her teacher had said that it might be a good idea for the sixth formers to read the cards, or at least to be ready to help with the reading. She remembered it now, rather too late.

'OK, Mark,' she said. 'I'll read the card.'

There was no response. Mark was really crying now, with his head down. The whole thing was too much for him. He just wanted to be back at school with his own teacher.

Daljit put the card down. 'OK, Mark,' she said. 'Forget the card. Tell me what's up.'

Mark lifted his head up and sniffed a bit. 'I didn't want to come,' he said. 'I knew it would be hard. I knew I wouldn't be able to do it. I'm not very good at reading. I have to have special help.'

He was going to say that other children sometimes made fun of him, but he couldn't bring himself to say it.

'Well,' said Daljit, 'I think the point is that I'm supposed to help you. I haven't done very well so far though. In fact, I've made a big mess of it.'

Mark smiled at that. Daljit saw the smile, and decided to build on it a bit.

'When it comes to finding the work hard,' she said, 'I could tell you a thing or two. Shall I tell you?'

Mark nodded. Daljit went on.

'When I first came here, we'd just moved house into the area. In the school I went to before there were lots of kids from all different countries. I felt quite at home, really.

'Then I landed here in this school with no other Asian kids in it at all. I just remember all these white faces and fair hair all around me, everywhere I looked. Some of them were unkind to me as well.'

'Unkind how?' asked Mark, who was becoming interested.

'Oh, they called me the usual names, that sort of thing,' she said. She laughed when she said it, but there was a hint of pain in her eyes.

In the science lab

'I didn't tell my mum. She had enough problems settling in at home, and learning her new job and trying to improve her English.'

'But you could read,' said Mark.

Daljit nodded. 'I could read and write very well. But there were still things I couldn't understand. I remember, in English we were working on instructions for making tea. I couldn't make head or tail of it. In our house we'd never made tea in the way the other kids were describing. It sounded ridiculous to me. And when I tried to explain, the other kids laughed and made fun. The teacher told them off, but it didn't make a lot of difference. I was the odd one out.'

The odd one out. Mark thought about that. He felt a bit like that sometimes. He had a real problem with his reading and writing, and it made him feel like the odd one out.

'Did it get any better?' he asked Daljit.

'Oh yes,' said Daljit. 'The school realised that it had to work on the attitudes of the other kids. And the other kids realised that I was OK really. Gradually I made some friends. I still get the odd remark, but I'm a sixth former now – older, more confident. I know I'm as good as most and a lot better than some. I'm brilliant at science – as I was supposed to show you today!'

They both laughed. Daljit picked up the workcard and laid it on the bench between them. She picked up a pencil and put it on the first word. 'I'll read,' she said. 'You follow.'

✦ Conclusion

Mark and Daljit were very different in some ways – from different kinds of homes, in different schools, very different in age.

But they had something in common. Daljit had once felt cut off from the other children – an odd one out. Mark was feeling that, too. They were able to share their feelings with each other.

That's an important part of making any kind of partnership with another person, or working together with someone else. There's more to it than just doing the job. You learn things about each other, and you learn to support each other.

☼ A prayer

Lord, help us to be able to see what our friends are feeling, so that we can say the things that are helpful to them. Make us sensitive and unselfish in all our relationships in school and at home. Amen.

☼ A thought

A problem shared is a problem halved.

Song suggestions

'When I needed a neighbour', *Someone's Singing Lord*, 35

'I will always be there', *Primary Assembly Song Book*, 40

Optional follow up

Ask the children to imagine you put them into threes to do some work. What do they think they could bring to the group? A sense of humour? The ability to write quickly? Good listening? Ask them to write down what they think they each could contribute.

Fire, water and food

Assembly 1 of 4

Famine is not a simple issue. It is not just a lack of food, but is linked with a range of difficulties, as this assembly tries to show. Often, long-term difficulties need to be resolved to prevent future problems.

You will need

- some colourful books from the library
- a jug and a drinking glass
- a large container of water (25 litres if possible)
- some natural-looking firewood or some off-cuts
- a blank OHT and pens.

Taken by ....

Date ....

Given to ....

Comments

- ....
- ....
- ....

✦ Introduction

Are we rich here? Are we rich in this school? Generally, we don't think so. We have fundraising events to help us to buy things. We tell you to be careful with books and materials because we haven't got much money to spend on them. And yet if we really think about it, we are rich in all sorts of ways compared with so many other places. *(Hold up the books.)* Look at these lovely books. In many parts of the world, books are poorly printed, on thin paper, with no pictures in them. The children are eager to learn and would love books like these.

✦ Activity

Now let's think about India. Who'll come to the front and be an Indian school for me?

Invite ten pupils to the front. Stand them in a line. Get them to make a roof with their hands at face level, so that each child represents a school.

Here are ten schools in India. *(Count them off.)* One, two, three, four, five, six, seven, eight, nine, ten.

Now, out of every ten schools in India, four have no proper building – just very rough temporary huts, or perhaps just a simple shelter.

Get four children to put their 'roof' hands down by their sides. Then make the ten roofs again.

Out of every ten schools in India, four have no blackboard.

Again, four children put their hands down.

Make the roofs again.

Out of every ten schools in India, six have no drinking water.

Again, indicate by putting hands down

Let's think about drinking water for a moment. First, all that talk has made me feel like a drink of water myself.

Fire, water and food

(Pick a child.) (Name), I want a drink of water. Can you take this jug and fill it with water please? We'll all wait while *he/she* does that. (*Time how long this takes – not openly, in case the child runs. Remember the time for later.*)

There, that didn't take long did it? Where did you have to go? That's not far is it?

Can you pour me a glass of water? Now I'm going to have a drink. I know the water is fine to drink. We all have water on our dinner tables at school. Some of you put your heads under the tap to have a drink.

What must it be like to have no drinking water in school? Remember, six out of ten schools in India have no drinking water laid on. That means their water has to be brought in, carried in barrels or other containers. They have to look after it and not waste it.

The drinking water problem is the same all over the world – let's think about Africa for example.

📖 Reading

There are many parts of Africa where the men have to leave home to go hundreds of miles away to work in cities or down mines. Let's think about one woman – we'll call her Sofie.

Her husband has gone off to work in the mines, five hundred miles away. He only gets home on very special occasions. In the meantime these are some of the jobs she has to do.

- Look after the crops.
- Look after the animals.
- Collect water.
- Collect firewood.
- Make a cooking fire.
- Look after the children.

To get through all this work she has to get up at five o'clock every morning, and she won't finish until half past nine at night.

Why should it be such hard work, you wonder? I'll tell you just two reasons. First, there is water. How long did it take (*name*) to get me a jug of water? I'll tell you, because I timed *him/her*. It took exactly…

Now Sofie, on the other hand, has no water in her own village. Long ago there used to be a well, but it dried up. Now, she has to walk to get it. She walks five kilometres there, and five kilometres back. (*Illustrate if you can – 5 kilometres is about 3 miles.*)

That's like the distance from here to…
It takes her an hour to get there, and an hour to get back.

But that's not all. A lot of women go to the well, so she usually has to queue for two hours. So she is away from home for four hours just to get water.

Would she just carry a jug, do you think, like the one that (*name*) brought me?

No, if she's going to be away for four hours, she's got to make it worthwhile. She has to bring enough water for her four children and herself and her mother-in-law.

In the dry season, she might need enough water for her animals as well. So she'll carry as much as she can, in two buckets on a pole across her shoulders. She'll carry about twenty-five litres altogether. That's how much I've got in this container. Who'll come and try its weight?

Would you like to carry that in the heat of the African sun, on a dusty day, for five kilometres – a brisk hour's walk?

Fire, water and food

And yet water is so important if Sofie and her family are going to be healthy. So many diseases thrive when there is no clean water. The shortage of water causes all sorts of problems. But it takes up precious time that Sofie could be using for other jobs, or for talking to her children and teaching them. That's not the end of it, though. *(Hold up the firewood.)*

Second, if Sofie is to light a fire and cook food, then she has to gather firewood. Wood is a very important source of fuel in the Third World – eight people out of ten in the Third World depend on wood for fuel for cooking and for heating.

In many parts of Africa there is a shortage of firewood. This is because so much wood has been used. In some places, huge amounts of wood have been used by industry.

And as the population increases, more wood is needed for firewood. At the same time, more forest is cleared for farmland, so there are fewer trees. There is a firewood crisis in Africa.

The loss of trees also causes other problems, because trees hold water in the soil, support wildlife, act as windbreaks and stop the soil from being blown away by the wind.

So, Sofie spends three hours every day gathering wood for her cooking fire. All the time she has to go further and further for scraps of wood.

All of these things threaten people's lives. Without water, crops, animals and people die. The more time people spend on fetching water and wood, the less time they have to care for crops and animals. As trees disappear, soil is blown away and grows poorer crops.

So you see, if we are going to help the people in lands where there is famine, we need to do more than just send parcels of food. Sending the food is helpful for saving lives but we need to do more.

There are people who are trying to help, of course.

Voluntary Service Overseas sends out people to work all over the world, helping to educate people, and helping to make better use of resources.

The Intermediate Technology Development Group helps people in the Third World to use what they have more efficiently. For example, they are helping the firewood crisis by helping to develop better cooking stoves which do not use so much wood.

WaterAid helps with digging wells and with other methods of bringing fresh water to Third World villages.

✦ Poem

This poem has a repeated line, for the pupils to join in. The line is 'We're thinking of you, and reaching out to help'.

Our brothers and sisters in India
Trying hard to learn
In schools with no walls
No water; no blackboard.
We admire you.
We can learn from your enthusiasm.
We're thinking of you, and reaching out to help.

Our sisters in Africa
Working so hard
Walking miles for water
Walking miles for wood.
We admire you.
We can learn from your determination.
We're thinking of you, and reaching out to help.

Fire, water and food • page 3 of 4

131

Fire, water and food

Our brothers and sisters all over the world
You are in our thoughts
We want you to succeed
To have schools, fresh water,
And wood to cook with.
And enough food to eat.
We're thinking of you, and reaching out to help.

☀ A prayer

Dear God, we remember all people, in this country and across the world, who find life a struggle. People who have to struggle for food, search for firewood, walk a long way for water. Help them, and help us to learn from their determination to succeed – so much that is true and inspiring has come from Africa and India, and we are grateful.

We remember, too, all those people who are working to solve Third World problems. (Mention anyone known – a former pupil on VSO or someone connected with the local church, maybe.) Amen.

☀ A thought

We all have bad days. There are people in this hall whose lives are not so happy at the moment. Of course we remember them. But today we want to spend a little time thinking about people across the world who have to struggle every day just to keep alive. At least not many of us in this country have that problem. Let's not forget. Let's do what we can to help.

Song suggestions

'The family of man', *Come and Praise*, 71

'Guantanamera', *Alleluya*, 11

'When I needed a neighbour', *Come and Praise*, 65

Optional follow up

As a follow-up activity, the pupils, with the help of teachers, can write to the named organisations for information. Each is a charity, so don't forget to send a big stamped, self-addressed envelope.

Contact details

Intermediate Technology Development Group

The Schumacher Centre for Technology and Development
Bourton Hall
Bourton-on-Dunsmore
Rugby CV23 9QZ
Tel: 01926 634400
Web: www.itdg.org

Voluntary Service Overseas

317 Putney Bridge Road
London SW15 2PN
Tel: 020 8780 7200
Web: www.vso.org.uk

WaterAid

Prince Consort House
27–29 Albert Embankment
London SE1 7UB
Tel: 020 7793 4500
Web: www.wateraid.org.uk

Helping

Assembly 2 of 4

This is an assembly for juniors about helping. It makes the point that being serious about helping means thinking your actions through, and not being put off if actions are met with apparent ingratitude, or if the jobs are unpleasant.

You will need

- an empty box – large but capable of being carried by one person

Taken by	....	....	....
Date	....	....	....
Given to	....	....	....

Comments

● ....

● ....

✦ Introduction

Pick up a box at one side of the hall and carry it to the other. Pretend that it is very heavy. Say things to reinforce this, and generally do some puffing and panting.

I might have to carry that box back again at the end of assembly. I might have to ask some people to help me. I wonder if anyone will volunteer to help me?

Lots of children will, of course, volunteer.

Ah yes. You all want to help. But I wonder if you would help if the job was really, really difficult? Or if things kept going wrong? Would you?

Here's a story about some girls who wanted to help but found that things were really difficult.

📖 Story

Mr Graham was sitting at home at about four in the afternoon watching the television when the doorbell rang.

'What on earth's that?' He said it out loud even though there was nobody to hear. A lot of people who spend time alone speak aloud instead of in their heads. It doesn't mean they're strange, it's just a habit they get into.

He struggled up out of his chair with the help of the walking stick he kept by his side. 'I'm coming!' he shouted rather crossly. And he made his way painfully to the door. He opened it cautiously without unfastening the chain, and looked through the crack. There were three schoolgirls there, giggling and fidgeting. Mr Graham saw them nudge each other when he looked at them. This annoyed him, because he didn't like people laughing at him. Sometimes when he went out, he thought that people were laughing at him because he had this habit of muttering to himself a bit.

'What do you want?' he said. He was rather cross, and he made it show in his voice.

The three girls looked at each other and then just collapsed in giggles again. Mr Graham swore to himself and shut the door. As he made his way across the hall, the doorbell rang again. He sighed and turned round. As he turned, he leaned against the wall and accidentally dropped his stick. It took him some time to pick it up again, and while he

Helping

was struggling, the doorbell rang yet again. By this time, Mr Graham was really annoyed. He said to himself, 'If it's those girls again, I'm going to give them a piece of my mind.'

He opened the door on the chain again and peered through. Sure enough it was the same three girls. One of them stepped forward and started to say something, but Mr Graham didn't wait. 'Be off with you! Fancy coming and annoying an old man! I've had enough. Off you go. Go and do something useful. Run off!' he shouted. And he closed the door again with a bump.

He stood for a moment to see if the girls were going to ring the bell again, but they didn't so he went slowly into the living room. Just to be sure, he went to the net curtains and lifted them to look through. The girls were standing by the pavement looking his way. One of them shouted something, and Mr Graham waved his walking stick at them and dropped the curtain.

'Young devils!' he said. 'I don't know what this place is coming to.'

Earlier that day, at Marston Street School, Mrs Duvall had been talking to her class about helping people. 'There are lots of people you can help,' she had said. 'I know some of you help your elderly neighbours to do the shopping. Old people really like it when younger people do jobs for them. Sometimes jobs that are easy for you are difficult when people are a bit older and not so steady on their feet.'

After the lesson, Nutan and Karen and Wilma had a little meeting on the playground. 'Let's help somebody!' said Karen. 'We could help an old person to do their shopping.'

'Right!' said Karen. 'But who can we help?'

Nutan had the answer, 'I know. We'll go to see Mr Graham at the end of our road!' The other

girls didn't know Mr Graham. They asked who he was.

'He's an old man. He lives on his own. He's a bit peculiar you know. Talks to himself,' Nutan explained.

Karen didn't like the sound of that. 'I'm not sure we should be going there,' she said.

'It'll be fine!' said Nutan. 'What can he say? He obviously needs help, and we're going to offer. He'll be really grateful.'

So, at four o'clock that afternoon the three girls stood outside Mr Graham's house. They were nervous about ringing the bell, so they kept trying to persuade each other to do it. This made them start giggling. One by one they kept going up to the door and then turning away. In the end, Nutan just went up and pressed the bell. The other two gave little giggly screams and they all stood back to see what would happen.

It seemed ages before anybody came. Nutan was just going to press the bell again when they heard rattling behind the door, and somebody talking in a grumbly voice. This set them off giggling again, and when the door opened a crack and the face of an old man peeped through, they were too giggly to speak properly. The old man looked funny peeping through the door, and he sounded quite cross. The girls looked at each other, and tried to control themselves. It took them a moment, and Karen was just going to answer the old man when they all just collapsed with the giggles. The old man shouted at them and shut the door.

The girls pulled themselves together. 'Come on!' said Nutan. 'We've got to do this properly. I'll ring the bell again, and this time when he comes, you two keep quiet and I'll go up the steps so he can hear me and I'll ask him if he'd like us to do any shopping for him.'

Helping

So Nutan rang the bell again. Once more, it was a long time before there was any answer, and the girls could hear thumps and bangs from inside the house. All this, combined with the long wait, was too much, and they just set off giggling again. When the door eventually opened. Nutan did manage to step forward, but before she could say anything, the old man just shouted to them to go away, and then slammed the door.

'Well!' said Karen. That's nice, isn't it? We've come to help and we get the door slammed in our faces.'

The girls stood on the pavement, grumbling to each other about people being ungrateful. They saw Mr Graham open the curtains, and Karen made one last attempt. 'We've come to help you with your shopping!' she shouted. But the old man just shook his stick at them and went back into the living room.

'That does it!' said Karen. 'You won't catch me trying to help anybody again. Wait till I tell Mrs Duvall!'

Next day, in class, when she had the chance, Karen put up her hand. 'You know what you were saying about helping people, Miss? Well, we tried to help somebody, and it didn't work. They didn't want helping at all. This old man just shouted at us to go away.'

Mrs Duvall looked at Karen, and decided that this was something that had to be looked into. She found out from Karen who else was involved and then arranged to see the three girls, with Mr Courtney, the head, at break.

'Right!' began Mr Courtney. 'Talk to me. Tell me what you've been up to.'

The girls were a bit miffed by this. They didn't think they had been 'up to' anything. They thought they had been doing something helpful, and they explained the whole thing.

'And he didn't want any help from us,' Karen said at the end of the story. He just told us to go away. He wasn't a bit grateful!'

Mr Courtney knew this would need careful handling, and he thought a bit before he spoke.

'I'm really glad that you wanted to help Mr Graham,' said Mr Courtney. 'I know him. He has been here for some of the Christmas plays you know. His daughter came here before she grew up and moved away. That was long before my time though.

'I want to tell you one or two things that will make it easier next time. Here are some rules. When I've finished I'd like you to write them out. Do it on the computer, and we'll make sure they are OK and then we can use them for anybody else who wants to help old people.

'Right. First, nobody, least of all young people like yourselves, should go knocking on anybody's door without warning. You know the rules about keeping yourselves safe. Did your parents know where you were? Did you have permission to go to the shops?

'And Mr Graham also knows that he has to be careful about who comes to his door. Think about it and you'll agree with me. Right? That's the most important thing.

'Second, you can't just turn up with difficult questions. If anybody came to me and asked if I wanted shopping doing, I wouldn't be able to answer. I'd need some time to think what I wanted so that I wasn't wasting anybody's time.

'Third, when we've done all that, and you do eventually get to see somebody, you have to be polite. You don't go giggling and fooling about – even if you didn't mean it. It puts people's backs up.

'Fourth, people are quite proud. They aren't going to say yes eagerly to everyone just

Helping

because help is offered. They need to be approached properly and given the chance to discuss things a bit. They even need the opportunity to refuse if it suits them. Or they may want you to do something else. Suppose he had said that he didn't want any shopping doing, but he would quite like some weeding doing in the garden?

'Helping, you see, isn't always easy. Helping can mean working with difficult people. It may mean doing things you don't like. It's not just doing comfortable things in nice places with grateful people. Think about the people who help others every day. They have to be prepared to do unpleasant jobs with people who have forgotten how to say thank you, or whose lives are so depressing that they are bad tempered all the time. If you want to do some helping like that, then the best thing is to come to your teacher or to me, and we'll see if we can work something out.

'Now, Mr Graham is a bit bad tempered. He has the right to be. He lives alone. He's had a hard life and his leg hurts him all the time. He might snap at you. He might still tell you to go away. If you go shopping for him, he might tell you off for bringing the wrong things, even if you bring exactly what he says. He might argue about the amount of change you've got. His house smells a bit because he finds it very difficult to keep it clean. He often forgets things. He might forget who you are when you go a second time.

'Now. The question is, do you still want to help Mr Graham?'

The girls had a good think, but Nutan knew what needed to be said, 'Yes, Mr Courtney. Sorry we didn't think about it properly. But we'd still like to help. Wouldn't we?' The other two girls nodded.

'Right!' said Mr Courtney. 'Leave it to Mrs Duvall and me. We have some notes to write, and I'll speak to your parents and to social services, and we'll do the job properly this time.'

Over the year the girls helped Mr Graham many times. They found out that Mr Courtney was right – Mr Graham was difficult sometimes, but they enjoyed the challenge of helping him feel better.

☀ A prayer

Dear God, help us to remember that you want us to help all people who are in need of help. We ask for your strength in facing up to unpleasant jobs and in facing up to people who are embarrassed or difficult. We ask that we can show your love to all the people we meet. Amen.

☀ A thought

How much do you love your friend? Could you wipe horrible, smelly mud off them with your own best handkerchief if they fell down in a ditch? Do you need people to say thank you, or can you give help for its own sake?

Song suggestions

'The best gift', *Come and Praise*, 59

'This little light of mine', *Alleluya*, 14

Precious resources

Assembly 3 of 4

This assembly for Christian Aid Week focuses on young children working in the developing world and how some Christian Aid projects are directed towards improving these children's lives.

You will need

- nothing at all.

Taken by	....	....	....
Date	....	....	....
Given to	....	....	....

Comments

- ....
- ....
- ....

✦ Introduction

Every country has resources of some kind which help it to survive – crops that grow, animals that can be reared for food, minerals under the ground such as coal, iron or oil.

Some of these resources can be used directly – a family can grow food and eat it, for example. Usually, though, the resources have to be sold or exchanged.

In our own country, the people who make cars don't take them home to keep. If they did, they would end up with a back garden full of cars! That would be useless because the family would have plenty of cars but no money.

So what happens is that the cars are sold and some of the money is paid to the workers. The workers then buy food and clothing with the money.

What do you think the most precious resource is in any country?

Is it diamonds like they have in South Africa? Or oil like they have in Saudi Arabia?

Is it coffee plantations like they have in Central and South America? Or tea plantations like the ones in India and Sri Lanka?

Well diamonds, oil, coffee and tea are all valuable resources. They can all be sold for money to help the people of the country to live.

Yet if you ask the people in a country what is the most precious thing they have, they probably won't say any of these things.

What they will say is that the most precious thing is their children.

Why do they say that?

It isn't just that people love their children. Although they do of course.

It's because children are a country's future.

If you look after children, educate them well and keep them healthy, the country stands a chance of having good workers and leaders in the future.

That is one of the reasons that you are so important to us.

Precious resources

In some countries, though, there is so much poverty that children have to work to help to support the family.

This is bad for a number of reasons.

It robs children of the chance to play and have a happy childhood.

It might make them unhealthy, so that they can't live a full adult life.

It makes it difficult for them to get a good education.

If a poor country is going to improve, it has to make sure that the children grow up healthy and educated.

Let me tell you two stories.

📖 Story 1

Let me tell you about Chela Maria Padilla.

Chela is ten. Who here is ten?

What time do you get up in the morning?

Take some responses.

Chela Maria gets up at five o'clock for part of the year.

That's because she lives on a coffee farm. Did you know that coffee grew on farms?

Coffee is made from coffee beans, which grow on bushes. The beans have to be picked by hand.

Chela's mum and dad both do the picking and she and her brothers and sisters have to help.

If they didn't help, the family wouldn't make enough money to live.

So, Chela gets up at five, helps her mum with the housework, then goes off to do a day's work picking and sorting coffee beans.

The trouble is that families such as Chela's – and there are many like them around the world – don't get much money for their crops.

The big companies pay Chela's family a very low price for the coffee beans which they then turn into the coffee in jars and packets that we are used to seeing.

There are companies though, like Cafedirect, which make sure that the farmers are paid a fair price for their crops.

So if you see Cafedirect coffee in the shop, at least give it a try, because you will be helping the families of people like Chela.

If they can earn a bit more money, perhaps the children will be able to spend more time on their education.

This will give them a better life and be better for their country too.

Let me tell you about another little girl, called Jeylakashmi, who is also ten.

📖 Story 2

Jeylakashmi lives in southern India. She goes to school and she enjoys her work.

Luckily, her school is near to her home, so she can easily get home at lunch time.

What does she do when she goes home do you think? Does she have a nice lunch and rest in front of the television?

No, she works at making matchboxes from flat pieces of card. She folds them up and sticks them together.

Jeylakashmi also gets up at seven every morning to make matchboxes before school.

After school, she goes home and makes even more.

Precious resources

She can make 1 000 matchboxes in one day.

Jeylakashmi can't just give up making the matchboxes because the family needs the money she makes. The money helps to buy the food and pay the rent.

Her father sells bread in the market, but he earns very little at this. So it looks as if Jeylakashmi might have to give up school too.

This would be a tragedy for her, because she likes school and is learning a lot.

She knows that if she does well at school, she will be able to get a better job than matchbox-making when she leaves.

✦ Conclusion

Both Chela Maria Padilla and Jeylakashmi are being helped by Christian Aid.

This is because Christian Aid helps organisations that try to keep children at school and cut down on their working hours.

Christian Aid tries to help people in poor countries in many ways.

They don't just give money. They arrange it so that people find a way to help themselves – to find a solution and to improve their own lives.

Children are very important to Christian Aid, because they see them as the future.

They know that people can only be helped if they are given the education and chances to help themselves.

Do you value your own education? I hope so. You are our country's future.

If our country is to improve in all ways, with better industry, better music and art, better sport, kinder attitudes and care for people who cannot care for themselves, then only you can do it.

When we are gone, you will take over. Then all that you have learned will be valuable to you.

That's the same in every country in the world.

☀ A prayer

Dear God, we remember the children of the world who live hard lives. Children who have too much to do and too little food. May we never forget that there are things we can do to help – by supporting Christian Aid and by buying products from firms that give families a fair price for their crops. Amen.

☀ A thought

If you had nothing at all, perhaps I could choose to give you one of two things. Perhaps I could give you fifty pounds. Or perhaps I could give you, instead, a piece of land, a spade and some seeds. Which would be better? Think about it.

Song suggestions

'This starving Earth', *Primary Assembly Song Book*, 17

Optional follow up

- You could contact Christian Aid at 35 Lower Marsh, London SE1 Tel: 020 7620 4444 Fax: 020 7620 6719.

- Write diaries for Chela Maria Padilla and Jeylakashmi – finding out more about where they live and giving their hopes for the future.

- Ask the children to write a piece suggesting ways in which both the farmers and the manufacturers might be satisfied.

Captain Scott and Captain Oates

Captain Scott and Captain Oates

Assembly 4 of 4

This assembly tells of Scott's expedition and particularly of the sacrifice of Captain Oates.

You will need

- a globe (a large ball will do)

- OHT 1 provided on page 140.

- OHT 2 provided (optional) on page 144.

✦ Introduction

In today's assembly we are going to hear about two remarkable men who did something that we may find difficult to imagine.

Is anybody cold? I'm certainly not. It's quite warm in here really. But does anybody remember being really cold? Just for a moment, try to think about when you were really cold.

Let me tell you about a very, very cold place and about heroic people who went there on purpose, knowing that they would suffer, but hoping that out of their suffering would come great things – discoveries and the sense of achievement.

We use the expression 'the ends of the Earth', but what does it mean?

The Earth, after all, is a sphere. Like this.

Hold up the globe or ball.

It doesn't actually have any ends, does it?

In one sense the Earth does have ends in the form of its poles – the far north and the far south at the ends of its rotational axis.

Demonstrate with the globe or ball.

The power of the sun is weak at the poles. There are long days in the summer, but it is still very cold. The winters are dark and savagely cold.

Travelling to the poles is still difficult. Even today, anyone who has been there has done something very special.

So it was that in the year 1910, some brave and adventurous men – and they were all men, because in those days there were not so many women explorers – set out to reach the South Pole.

There were two expeditions, each hoping to be first. One was led by Roald Amundsen and one was led by Captain Scott.

The story is well known. You can read it in great detail for yourself. What I want to do now, though, is to take you to how it finished for Captain Scott. Here he is.

Put up OHT 1 provided.

Captain Scott and Captain Oates

📖 Story

Scott and his team reached the South Pole, after a nine-hundred mile trek across the ice, only to find that Amundsen had got there before him.

What a crushing blow that was – to make that dreadful journey across the ice, up the glaciers and along the polar plateau, only to find that he was not first.

The return was a desperate struggle. One man, Edgar Evans, died.

Then the remaining four, Henry Bowers, Edward Wilson, Scott and Captain Lawrence Oates, struggled on until dreadful weather forced them to stop and take shelter in a tent.

They never managed to get any further. They all died in the tent, trapped by the weather and their weak condition, short of food and exhausted by their struggle.

What everyone remembers, though, is the action of Captain Lawrence Oates.

Oates was in a worse condition than the others. He was suffering from frostbite and was very weak.

He worried that he was holding the others up, that they might be able to get to safety but for his weakness.

So as they lay in their tent, with the wind howling outside, Oates made a decision.

He stood up and said, 'I am going outside and I may be some time.'

He knew, and the others knew, that he would not be coming back. He was going out to die in the snow. He gave his life in the hope that his friends would be able to move on without him.

Alas, it was not to be. The weather was still too bad for the others to go on and they died in their tent some days later.

How do we know all this? Almost to the very end, Captain Scott kept a diary, in which he wrote all these things. Towards the end, in that dark and lonely tent, with the gale howling outside, he wrote, by the dim and flickering light of a lamp.

'I do not regret this journey, which has shown that Englishmen can endure hardships, help one another, and meet death with as great a fortitude as ever in the past. We have been willing to give our lives for this enterprise, which is for the honour of our country.'

Optional
Put up OHT 2 provided and read the poem.

✦ Conclusion

Jesus said, 'Greater love hath no man than this, that a man give up his life for his friends.'

That's what Captain Oates did, of course. He chose to die in order to give his friends a chance to survive.

Could you do that, do you think? It's one of those questions that you can't answer. Nobody knows what they would do. Only when it happens can you make the decision. All we know is that there are plenty of examples like this.

Captain Scott and Captain Oates

Jesus spoke of the great love that will lead to a person giving up his life, when he was giving a long talk to his closest followers.

He spoke about his love for them and, time and time again, he urged them to love each other.

'Continue in my love,' he said. 'This is my commandment, that you love one another as I have loved you.'

Jesus wanted his disciples to stay together and support each other through thick and thin.

Can you imagine Oates, Scott, Wilson and Bowers in the last days of their journey? Do you think they got impatient with one another? Of course they did.

Did they get fed up with each other's little habits or with bigger problems, such as Oates' inability to walk quickly? Of course they did. But they stuck together. They kept their feelings under control.

That's what Jesus wanted his disciples to do — to stick together and keep their feelings under control by remembering their love for each other.

In school we can all stick together, be patient with one another, help each other, accept each other and be prepared to give time and effort to each other.

Oates was special for all the best reasons — he was brave and unselfish. And because of that he became famous after his death.

☀ A prayer

Dear God, we thank you for the lives of all those who have set examples of courage and self-sacrifice. Help us to have some of the same courage so that when things go wrong we may still be able to think of others and put their needs before our own. Amen.

☀ A thought

The real test of friendship is when you have to put your friend's needs and wishes first, and give up something yourself. Can you pass that test?

Song suggestions

'He who would valiant be', *Come and Praise,* 44

'He is there', *Primary Assembly Song Book*, 35

Optional follow up

Map out the trek that Scott and the others made and display it along with their story.

Captain Scott and Captain Oates

Oates stepped out

And the freezing wind

Cut through to his very soul.

It sang the terrible song they had heard

All the way back from the Pole.

Oates stepped out

Into driving snow

And the fearsome polar night.

His heart weighed down and hopeless

But sure what he did was right.

Oates stepped out

And screwed up his eyes

To look through the blinding storm.

And fancied he saw someone waiting there

To guide him safely home.

Captain Scott and Captain Oates

The Winter Boy

Assembly 1 of 4

This is a Christmas assembly. Christmas is a time when we think of giving and receiving because it is a birthday – Jesus', and a time of great celebration for Christians. People of other religions often like Christmas, too, because of all the good things that happen, and because it is a time of love and joy and understanding between people. This is a story about a mysterious event one Christmas, with a starry jewel, a theft, and the strange Winter Boy.

You will need

- nothing at all.

Taken by ....

Date ....

Given to ....

Comments

⊙ ....

⊙ ....

⊙ ....

📖 Story

The boy walked by the window again. Jacquie looked up from the starry jewel in her hand and wondered for the hundredth time what he was doing out there. His hair was waxed into spikes, his eyes were sad, and although his feet weren't bare, the old trainers wouldn't last much longer. In spite of the cold, all he was wearing was an out-of-date football top and scruffy jeans.

She turned back to the jewel. She didn't know how much it had cost her father, but Jacquie's share had taken up half her savings. If you turned it to the left, it flashed lightly. If you turned it to the right, it sparkled. She would not wrap it until the last moment, just before she gave it to her mother on Christmas morning.

The room was ready for the evening of Christmas Eve, also her mother's birthday. Everything was covered in birthday cards and Christmas cards. The decorations glittered and thrilled Jacquie's heart as they always did, even

though she was nearly thirteen. Under the tree were the rest of the presents for Christmas Day, but Jacquie held the hard, cold starry jewel in her hand.

She had overheard her father on the phone to RentaSanta, and Father Christmas and his gnomes would be here soon.

Jacquie looked up. The boy was walking past the house again. He stared in, straight at the girl, just as she was holding the jewel up to the lights on the tree, to see what difference they made to it. He was thin and wiry, and about three years older than Jacquie. She got up suddenly, and closed the curtains with a swish, making sure they met neatly in the middle. Now everything was perfect. She put the jewel carefully in the little china pot on the mantelpiece in the hallway.

After tea, there was a knock on the door. There they were, the lot of them. No messing about having to come in and change, no unloading cases from a van. Certainly there was a van, but it was made up like a sleigh,

The Winter Boy

with a smiling fibre glass snowman on the top. Jacquie pretended she hadn't seen the word 'Nissan' on the front, where no sleigh would have a radiator grill, as this one did. A loudspeaker blared 'Jingle Bells' down the street, then stopped as the last gnome got out.

Father Christmas was just what you'd expect – fat as a beer barrel, red-cheeked, with a voice like the man who sat behind Jacquie at the football, only kinder and not so rough. 'Well! And where's the lucky lady then?' he bellowed, looking round the hallway. And all his gnomes echoed him. They were smaller men in green, one wearing, Jacquie noticed, with a tiny pang of disappointment, a digital watch, and LOVE and HATE tattoos on his fingers.

'Where's the lucky lady then? Where's the lucky lady then?' said the gnomes.

Behind them, in the street, the boy walked slowly past the open door.

The party was mad. They danced and drank fruit juice mixed with fizzy wine – even Jacquie had a little. They played musical laps, and Jacquie's mother fell off Father Christmas' knee, and laughed until she cried. Her father smiled on it all, joining in less, as was his way. He went into the kitchen once, and Jacquie heard him singing the new carol he had written for the college where he worked:

'The Winter Boy is waiting
In the winter cold
To tell again a story
You have often been told…'

Then there were jokes. 'What would you say to a little drink?' asked the gnome with the digital watch and the tattoos. 'Hello, little drink,' shouted Father Christmas, laughing.

They'd left the door slightly open and the boy still stood on the path outside, listening to the noise. Father Christmas and the gnomes

disappeared into the van for a moment, and then came back, dressed as clowns, spreading a surprisingly large tarpaulin over the living room carpet. They began clouting each other with wet sponges, mops, and the rest of a cleaner's gear. Then one gnome lifted up a bucket of water, held it dramatically in the air – tipped it – and a shower of newspaper clippings landed on the giggling Jacquie.

Outside, the boy inched closer to the open door.

'I'm going to get you,' he heard a raucous voice shout.

'Oh no you're not,' several similar, though less loud, voices replied.

He watched as visitors came – the vicar to wish Jacquie's Mum happy birthday, and to collect money for Crisis, the carol singers, the milkman with his bill. They went into the bright house for a moment, and re-appeared smiling, calling 'Happy Birthday! Happy Christmas!'

· · · · · · · · · · ·

Later, Jacquie was in bed. The party seemed to have been a success. She turned over, and put her hand under her pillow, and spread the fingers out, and thought about tomorrow. She could see the shape of her stocking at the end of the bed, and a small star was reflected in the dressing-table mirror through a chink in the curtains, which she hadn't completely closed. Even though the jokes were getting muddled in her head, she couldn't sleep.

She tried to think about wonderful things. That usually helped her get to sleep. In her head, Jason, of the Town side, scored. He dribbled round the goalkeeper, shot, and the ball was pulling the net back at the north end.

The Winter Boy

She won first prize at the dancing competition. Jason scored again, and waved in celebration – especially to her.

The light in the mirror reminded her of the starry jewel. She swung her legs silently on to the floor, felt around for her slippers, and put them on. She went quietly from the room, like a ghost in her long nightie, to the top of the stairs. She walked down into the dark living room, to look at the unlit tree, then back to the mantelpiece in the hall where she had put the starry jewel. She picked up the china pot. The jewel had gone.

It had been hard to wake her father. He'd had a long day at the college recording the carol service for the local radio, and the party had been tiring, what with all the preparations. Once Jacquie had woken him from the big bed where he lay with her sleeping mother, she gabbled out the story in whispers.

'Who could it be, Jacquie?' asked her father, his brow like a stave of music with no notes on it. 'Who's been in the house since you last saw it? Are you sure you haven't just lost it?'

They looked in the pot again. But why bother? thought Jacquie. I know it's not there. With sinking hearts, they went through all the people who'd called during the party. It was horrible to think of any of them as thieves – the vicar, the carol singers, the milkman.

Then Jacquie almost shouted, 'It's that boy! He's been there all evening! We left the door open, and he came in and nicked it!' Her father looked at her long and hard. 'You try to sleep now, and I'll phone the police in the morning.'

Somehow they did sleep, and early next day they told Mum that she'd have to wait for her special present. Jacquie's stocking had been delightfully full and lumpy with treasures. Their Christmas Day breakfast – toast and hot chocolate with Mars Bars dipped in it for Jacquie, poached eggs for her parents with the lovely smelling coffee from the new machine – cheered them up. So did the music from the radio.

Then Jacquie saw the boy again. He was still outside the house, still wearing his football top, still expressionless. Jacquie dashed out.

'Hey, you, you've got it, I know you have, give it to me, my mum's present, the best present ever.' She ran out of breath and paused. The boy just looked at her. By now her father had come up to them. 'Have you taken something from our house?' No answer. 'What's your name?'

'My name is Christopher,' the boy replied.

His jeans, Jacquie noticed, were almost covered in badges. Among the flags, the skulls and crossbones, the football team colours, was a metal star, shining dully like a cross.

'Where's my mum's present?' said Jacquie, recovering her breath. When there was no reply, her father said, 'Let's go inside.'

Her mum was gazing at them all, speechless from the armchair. The radio babbled on. The boy said nothing. And then the words came knocking at Jacquie's ear.

'Following a series of thefts at homes in the St Morwen's area last evening and during the night, police have arrested a man dressed as a gnome, with tattooed letters depicting love and hate on his fingers. It is believed that he found access to houses by…'

The Winter Boy

Jacquie didn't bother listening any more. She knew how he'd got into people's houses.

Later the four of them sat down to Christmas dinner. There was a strange contrast between the shining jewel on the woman's jacket, and the star on the boy's jeans. He was starry in other ways too – even his hair was like rays. His eyes looked straight at you when you asked him something, as if he had nothing to hide.

He'd examined carefully all the Christmas cards with Mary and Joseph and Jesus on them. Some he'd liked, it seemed, some he hadn't. Now, with his newly scrubbed hands, he picked up the bread and broke it and gave it to them.

They switched on the radio as a choir sang Dad's new carol, and they listened.

> 'The Winter Boy is waiting
> In the winter cold
> To tell again a story
> You have often been told…'

In the warm lit house, they ate and drank, and talked about everything under the stars, as if they'd been friends all their lives.

> 'The Winter Boy is waiting
> With His myrrh and His gold
> And the scent of incense
> In the winter cold.'

> Fred Sedgwick

✦ Conclusion

Who was the Winter Boy? Was Christopher the Winter Boy? Was Christopher, in some way, the Christ child? Who knows? And it's one of those stories where it doesn't really matter – you make of it what you want. The best stories are often like that.

 ## A prayer

Dear God, soon it will be the day of Christ's birth. Help us to remember that it is a time of love and of giving. A time when we welcome people into our hearts and our homes. A time when friends and families meet.

Let us remember the Winter Boy this Christmas. He was outside in the cold, suspected of bad things until the family welcomed him in. Let us remember all those who are homeless, all those who are out in the cold this Christmas, and all those who are unhappy when so many of us are celebrating. May we all welcome the Winter Boy into our hearts and homes. Amen.

A thought

Winter can be a gloomy time – the mornings are dark, and it's dark when we go home from school. But there are bright moments – good times here in school at Christmas, and in our homes. As we enjoy our good times, we ought always to remember people who only have the gloom and depression – homeless, sad and lonely people.

Let's be generous with our love and thoughtfulness on these dark winter days. Let's remember the Winter Boy.

Song suggestions

'A rose is sweet', *Alleluya*, 44

'Mary had a boy child', *Tinder Box*, 63

The Rosetta Stone

Assembly 2 of 4

This assembly is about writing as a code. It starts with an account of the unlocking of an unknown language – the story of the Rosetta Stone.

You will need

* the OHT provided.

Taken by ....

Date ....

Given to ....

Comments

⦿ ....

⦿ ....

⦿ ....

✦ Introduction

This assembly is about writing and the wonderful idea that marks on paper can be understood if you know what the marks mean. If you do not have the secret of what the marks mean, then you cannot understand the writing.

Suppose we found some writing from long ago, and we had no way of knowing what it meant. We would look at it and puzzle over it. But unless we found the key to the code, we might never know what the writing said.

That's how it used to be with ancient Egyptian picture writing – called hieroglyphics.

📖 Reading

Many examples of hieroglyphics survived, mostly because the ancient Egyptians locked up writings in their tombs, and also wrote the stories of their kings and princes on the walls of the tombs themselves.

People looked at these pictures and just knew that if they could understand them they would know much more about the Egyptians and how they lived. But they had no way of working out what the picture language meant – it was a forgotten language.

Then came a breakthrough. In 1799, some French soldiers were in Rosetta in Egypt when they discovered a black stone, beautifully carved with pictures and writing.

The British were fighting the French at the time, and when they defeated the French they took the stone, which went into the British Museum in London.

The experts looked at it and realised that it contained the key to reading hieroglyphics.

This was because it had three sets of writing on it. (*Put up OHT provided.*) One set was in hieroglyphics, another was in another Egyptian language, called 'demotics', and another was in Greek.

Now Greek was not a forgotten language. There were experts who could read it.

So there were these three pieces of writing, two in unknown languages, one in a known language.

The Rosetta Stone

How did the experts know that they were all on the same subject?

A language expert called Thomas Young made the crucial link.

First he noticed that in the Greek writing the name of the Egyptian emperor Ptolemy appeared six times.

Then when he looked at the hieroglyphics, he realised that one particular sign appeared six times, each time in more or less the same position in the hieroglyphic text as the word Ptolemy appeared in the Greek text.

This led him to believe that he had found the hieroglyphic that stood for 'Ptolemy'.

It also led him to believe that the hieroglyphic text and the Greek text were the same – one was a translation of the other.

So if he studied it, he would find other words that could be tracked from the Greek to the hieroglyphics, and gradually he would build up a list of hieroglyphic words that he knew the meaning of.

He would be rediscovering a lost written language.

That was only the beginning. Building up a whole language from what was a short passage was very difficult.

Hieroglyphics turned out to be a very complicated language – sometimes a particular sign or picture stood for a whole word, sometimes it just stood for one letter. It was not easy to see when it was one and when it was the other.

There was a lot more work to be done, but in the end the experts understood the written language of hieroglyphics almost perfectly.

✦ Conclusion

Can you imagine looking at a page of writing and not knowing what it means?

A written language can be a frustrating mystery, unless we have a way of understanding it. We can stare at the marks and symbols and try to see some sort of solution, but we do need a key. For our own language, we are given the key by our parents and families and our teachers as we grow.

Often we can learn the key to other languages in the same sort of way. But if there is no key, then we cannot understand. The Rosetta Stone was a key to unlock the understanding of a language.

☀ A prayer

Dear God, we thank you for the gifts of writing and reading. Help us to read with care and to write with thoughtfulness so that we can understand others and they can understand us. Amen.

☀ A thought

We all have the key to learning in the support of our friends, family and school.

Song suggestions

'World calypso', *Primary Assembly Song Book,* 59

'He's got the whole world', *Come and Praise,* 19

Hieroglyphics

Demotics

Greek

φιλοτησιαν προπιντω υμιν

Spiders' webs

Assembly 3 of 4

In this assembly, children notice the remarkable sight of the school field covered in spiders' webs – quite common on a dewy autumn morning. This leads them to talk to their teacher about spiders – some of the most remarkable creatures on the planet.

You will need

- nothing at all.

Taken by ....

Date ....

Given to ....

Comments

● ....

● ....

● ....

✦ Introduction

This assembly tells us about one of nature's cleverest engineers – the humble spider, who uses strong thread to build a web. We will learn a little about spiders and hear the story of Arachne, the spinner of Greek mythology

Do you like spiders? Don't worry. You're not alone if you don't. There's something about spiders that seems to worry a lot of us. In fact, so many people are afraid of spiders that there's a special name for it – arachnophobia. But more about that name later.

Actually it's not really fair of us to be afraid of spiders, because they really are the most amazing creatures, with skills and talents all of their own. The more you know about them, the more you wonder at the complicated and beautiful way our world and all the living things in it work together.

We come into contact with spiders in all sorts of ways. Sometimes we discover that they are living in the house with us, sharing its warmth and comfort without causing us any trouble.

Sometimes they get into trouble themselves of course. It's quite common to find a spider stuck in the bath or the sink, for example. Incidentally, don't make the mistake of thinking that he's come up the plug hole – how could he do that when the pipe's full of water? He's stuck in the bath because he's slipped in and can't get up the smooth sides to get out. If you're worried about finding a spider in the bath, just leave a towel on the edge hanging down inside, and you'll give him an escape ladder, and you'll probably never find a spider in the bath again.

They aren't just in the house of course. They are in the fields and woods and gardens – big ones four centimetres across, and little ones half a millimetre across, and every size in between. We have over six hundred kinds of spiders in this country. We don't notice them much because they're small and they get on with their business which doesn't have much to do with us. But sometimes something happens to make us notice them. Here's a story about a spider encounter at Sir Henry Beaumont Primary School.

📖 Story

'Sir! Sir! Come and look at the field!'

It was 8.30 in the morning, and Mr Harries, the head, was trying to catch up on his paperwork before school. He wasn't keen on being interrupted by two Year 5 children.

'Why would I want to look at the field?' he said. 'I've seen it before. I know where it is. I know what it looks like. It's green, with goalposts on it.'

'You haven't seen it like this, Sir,' said Wendy. 'You have to come and see.'

Sighing, Mr Harries saved the work he was doing on his computer and went outside. There he stopped, and sighed again, this time in astonishment and wonder, for the field, all the way between the edge of the playground and the hedge by the canal, was covered with a sort of shimmering misty haze, glistening in the morning autumn sunlight.

They stood looking for a while. 'What's doing it?' asked Wendy.

'It's spiders' webs,' said Mr Harries. 'The whole field is covered with fine spiders' webs. It always is at this time of the year.'

'But why haven't we seen them before?' asked Martin.

'It's the dew,' said Mr Harries. 'In the early morning, the water vapour in the air condenses out as drops of water on the cold ground and the grass. It's clinging to the spiders' webs in tiny droplets, and the sunlight is reflecting from them, so you get this lovely misty shimmering effect. It's one of the most wonderful sights in nature, I think.'

'But all those spiders!' said Wendy. 'There must be thousands!'

'Millions, I'd guess, on this whole field,' said Mr Harries. 'And enough small insects to feed them all – because that's what they live on. All spiders are carnivores. They catch insects then they nip them with their poisonous fangs.'

'Then they eat them,' said Wendy.

'Well…' said Mr Harries. 'Spiders can only take liquids. In a way, instead of plant eaters, or meat eaters, they are soup eaters. They turn the softer bits of the insect into a sort of soup by spitting digestive juices on it.'

Wendy went a shade of green, and Mr Harries laughed. 'Well I think that's clever. Digesting some of your food while it's still on your plate seems quite efficient to me. Don't try it at home though.'

'What about the webs,' asked Martin. 'They catch insects in them, don't they?'

'Well, they all spin silk,' said Mr Harries. 'But not all spiders use the silk to make webs. Sometimes they make nests for their home or for their eggs. Some spiders go prowling round looking for food. You're right, though, a lot of spiders make webs to catch insects. The insect blunders into the web and gets stuck because the silk is coated with sticky stuff. The spider feels the vibration and off it goes to where the insect is, and then it might wrap the insect up for later. Or it might do the soup-making trick.'

'Where does the silk come from?' asked Martin.

'That's the cleverest trick of all,' said Mr Harries. 'The spider produces a liquid protein inside its body and sends it out of spinnarets at the back. It turns into solid thread when it hits the air. The spider turns it out at high speed. It's almost unbreakable – you try to break it and it just keeps stretching. It's much stronger than a steel wire the same size.'

Spiders' webs

'Clever little insects,' said Wendy.

'No, not insects,' said Mr Harries. 'Never call a spider an insect. An insect has six legs and three parts to its body – head, thorax and abdomen. A spider has two parts to its body and eight legs. It's an arachnid. It also usually has eight eyes, and almost always has a pair of poisonous fangs for catching and paralysing the insects it needs for food.'

Down in the grass on the field, a tiny spider called Arachne was listening to Mr Harries.

'Not bad. Not bad at all,' she said to herself. 'But he's missed out the most important bit. Let's see if I can make him hear.'

Arachne focused her four pairs of eyes on the little group of people above her and tried to think herself into Mr Harries' mind. 'Mr Harries!' She thought. 'Tell them about me. Tell them about poor Arachne!'

The group turned away. Arachne, the little spider in the grass, returned to her spinning. 'Ah well,' she said to herself. 'Not many people know about me anyway. It would have been nice for those children to hear the story of Athene and Arachne. But I've got enough to do. Must get on. Must get on. Silk to weave, insects to catch, soup to make.'

Do you want to hear the story of Arachne, and how the spider learned to spin?

Long, long ago, said the Ancient Greeks, there was a goddess called Athene. The goddess Athene was in charge of art and craft, among other things. She was particularly proud of being able to spin fine thread, which she then made into beautiful flowing robes as gifts for her fellow goddesses.

'I'm the best spinner in the world,' she said. On Earth, though, many people were tired of the way the gods and goddesses were always boasting of their wonderful powers. So people sometimes tried to do better just to show that the gods and goddesses weren't all that they pretended to be.

So it was that a peasant girl called Arachne one day said to herself, 'The goddess Athene is always boasting about being able to spin fine thread. But I'm sure I can do just as well. I spin all the thread for the clothes for our family, and I'm pretty good at it by now.'

So she turned up on Mount Olympus, the home of the gods, one day and said, 'Athene, I, Arachne, can spin as well as you.'

Athene was really angry at this, and she challenged Arachne to a contest. The two of them sat at their spinning wheels and they span and span and span, the fine thread coming from their wheels and coiling at their feet.

In the end, some of the other gods and goddesses gathered round and said, 'Well, Athene, sorry to say that this girl's done pretty well. Yes, she's quite something is Arachne. Your thread's good, but you have to admit that hers is better.'

Now Arachne thought that Athene would be generous – she was a goddess after all – and would say 'well done' and ask her to stay on Olympus and give her some help.

No such luck. The Greek gods weren't a bit like that. They were generally grumpy individuals, and it wasn't a good idea to get on the wrong side of them. So Athene was really angry with Arachne and told her to go away and that she would be her enemy for ever.

Spiders' webs

This upset Arachne so much that, alas, she died of a broken heart.

Now it was Athene's turn to be upset. She wished that she had not lost her temper. She was so remorseful that she said that Arachne could return to Earth as a spider, and that for ever she would be able to spin finer thread than any human being ever could.

To this day, we remember Arachne's name because scientists say that spiders are members of the Arachnid family.

So when you see a spider spinning, and you see its beautiful and magical web, sparkling in the morning dew, remember poor Arachne, who annoyed a goddess, but was allowed to continue her spinning. Remember Arachne and don't harm the spider. Watch it closely, see the wonderful things that it can do. Examine its amazing web, try to look into some of its eight eyes and see whether it looks a bit like a peasant girl from Ancient Greece. Then move away and let it get on with what it has to do. Most importantly, if you find one in the house that you or someone else in the family doesn't like very much, then don't kill it but put it outside – the chances are it will soon find its way back in again anyway.

✦ Conclusion

Every day, if you look, you can be amazed by the natural world around. You can see the dance that the bees do to let the other bees know where nectar is to be found. You can see the bats using their astonishing echo locating system for making a mental sound picture of their surroundings. You can see dogs sniffing around and building a mental smell picture of their world. Sometimes it all seems cruel of course – the spiders trap the insects, the birds swoop on the spiders, the cats and hawks try

to catch the birds. But it all fits together in a wonderful way. And we as human beings are privileged not just to see all this but to be part of it. We have the power, too, to preserve it all or destroy it. We should pray that we can keep the wonderful world in the way that God intended.

☀ A prayer

O Lord, we thank you for the wonders of nature, from tiny organisms that we cannot see to great whales voyaging the oceans in search of food. Help us always to respect these beautiful creatures and the world that keeps them alive, for they are part of your creation. Amen.

☀ A thought

Don't go about without seeing. Take time to stop and study the world in which you live.

Song suggestions

'One forever,' *Primary Assembly Song Book* 2

'All creatures of our God and King' *Come and Praise* 7

Optional follow up

Not all spiders use their spinning abilities in the same way. Some build webs, others use their thread for other purposes. Can you find out the different ways that spiders use their spun thread?

The time for the healing of wounds has come.

The moment to bridge the chasms that divide us has come.

The time to build is upon us.

Let there be justice for all.

Let there be peace for all.

Let there be work, bread, water and salt for all.

Escape from captivity

Assembly 4 of 4

In this assembly, children are introduced to the idea that the performance and character of another human being can be awe-inspiring. It tells briefly of Nelson Mandela, and also tells some elements of the Bible story of Moses, whose leadership of the exodus from Egypt has been an inspiration for thousands of years.

You will need

- the OHT provided.

Taken by ....

Date ....

Given to ....

Comments

● ....

● ....

● ....

✦ Introduction

Optional

You can be inspired by wonderful people. In fact the longer you are on the Earth, growing up, the more you are amazed by the things that other human beings have done in their lives. It's a good thing to think about the achievements of great human beings, and to try to shape our lives in the same sort of way.

There are times when you look at something – a rainbow, perhaps, or a high-flying aeroplane heading off across the world – and it gives you a good feeling inside. You feel a little more cheered up, a little bit more ready to tackle the next job you have to do.

Some people have that same effect on you, of course. Perhaps you're feeling a bit down, and you're walking along going over your problems in your mind, and then coming towards you, you see a familiar face, someone you like, someone you admire. You're delighted to see this person and you start to smile, and your p

roblems disappear a little as you walk towards your friend, ready to listen to what they have to say.

What I want to talk about today, though, is the way that you can get a similar feeling from someone you don't know personally – a famous person perhaps, who you see in the distance on a stage, or on a sports field, or on the television. Just seeing that person reminds you of the wonderful things they have done, and remembering those things helps you face your own problems.

It might be a sports personality who has that effect – a once-great boxer like Muhammad Ali, who is now battling against a serious illness. Now when he appears on television, he isn't well enough to say much, but just to see him, and be reminded of his greatness gives millions of people a real lift of the spirit.

For many people, the great South African leader Nelson Mandela is like that. Just to see his photograph, or to see him on film is to be reminded of how he came from many years in prison to give wise leadership to his country.

Escape from captivity

📖 Story

Nelson Mandela was sent to prison in 1964. He came out in 1990. When he went in, South Africa was a divided country. Black people were treated badly by the white people who governed the country. There are far more black people than white people in South Africa, but for many years black people could not vote, and could not take part in governing their country. Schools for white children were better than schools for black children. Hospitals and houses for white people were better than those for black people. Nelson Mandela was one of the black leaders who fought against this. As a punishment he was sent to jail.

But while he was in jail, things gradually changed. The white government began to realise that it could not go on keeping black people out of power. A divided country is not a happy country. Any country needs the talents of all its people, all of whom should be treated equally and fairly in every way.

So in 1990, the white government let Nelson Mandela out of prison. It was the first step on the road to freedom. In 1994, when all people in South Africa, black and white, could vote, he became president of his country.

In many ways, the story of Nelson Mandela reminds us of the story of Moses in the Bible. He, too, was a great leader. He, too, led his people on a difficult journey from slavery and cruelty to new freedom.

So let's hear the story of Moses, as it might have been told by an old man remembering what Moses was like.

Do I remember Moses? Oh yes, I remember Moses. Anyone who met him never forgot him – those piercing eyes that looked into you until you felt uncomfortable. That way he had of picking up his walking stick and shaking it to emphasise what he was saying. And his anger. He was often an angry man. Be careful that you understand what I mean by that. It wasn't that he had a bad temper, or that he was sulky. Oh no. But he could be very angry with people who did wrong, or who were slow to understand what he was trying to say.

Moses became the leader of the Hebrew people – sometimes we call them the children of Israel, or the Israelites, but they are all names for the same people.

He led them at a difficult time, when they were travelling across the desert. It was a long, hot and difficult journey, and many of the people became impatient with him and with God. And while he was away from our camp, some of them made their own god – a calf made from gold. They asked everyone for any gold that they had and they made a golden calf and danced round it and worshipped it.

When Moses came back he became very angry. He threw down the golden calf and broke it up into little pieces, and he demanded that people follow him and the one true God.

Mind you, by then, he had already gone through some difficult times. Moses had led us all – all the children of Israel – out of Egypt where we had been slaves. He had visited the Pharaoh, the Egyptian ruler, time after time, saying 'Let my people go'. The Pharaoh didn't want to let us go, because he depended on us. We were the slaves who built his houses and his temples and palaces and pyramids. But in the end, after terrible things had happened to the Egyptian people – failed crops, diseases – he eventually did let us go, because he believed

Escape from captivity

that Moses, and God, were making these dreadful things happen. So we trekked across the desert in search of the promised land – the land that Moses said had been promised to us by God. Moses spent all of his life doing it.

Even his birth was a chancy business. He was lucky to be alive. He was born in Egypt, to a Hebrew woman. Now at that time the Israelite people were slaves in Egypt, cruelly treated. If new Hebrew babies were born, the Pharaoh was having them killed. So the story says that when Moses was born, his mother gave him a chance of life. She made a little boat from bulrushes, and put him in it, and sent him off to float down the river.

Soon the little boat came to rest in the reeds by the river. And who should find it there but the daughter of the Pharaoh? She looked in the little boat, and found the baby Moses. She knew it was a Hebrew baby, and she should have reported it. But the baby cried and looked up at her, and she could not bring herself to do anything to hurt him.

So it was that Moses was brought up by the Pharaoh's daughter, a Hebrew in the palace of the Pharaoh.

As Moses grew up, he realised that it would be his job to take the Hebrew people out of Egypt. He heard the voice of God talking to him and telling him to go to the Pharaoh and say 'Let my people go'.

So for many long and difficult years after that, the children of Israel travelled in the deserts, hoping to reach the land that God and Moses had promised to them.

It was an incredible achievement to my mind. He led this great number of people, keeping up their spirits, and keeping them together in times of great difficulty. There were arguments, and times when people lost faith in

God and Moses, but always he won out in the end, and kept the people focused on what they had to do, which was to make this great journey to a better life.

So Moses, you see, is an inspiration to me – an example of someone who did what seemed impossible. He led his people from slavery to freedom, keeping them together when their spirits were low, and always inspiring them to greater efforts. I would like to guess that for thousands of years people will remember Moses. Other leaders will come along – men and women who can lead their people from slavery to freedom – and whenever that happens, people will say, 'It reminds me of Moses'.

✦ **Conclusion**

When Nelson Mandela had led his country to freedom and became president of South Africa in 1994, he made a speech containing these sentences.

> 'The time for the healing of the wounds has come.
>
> The moment to bridge the chasms that divide us has come.
>
> The time to build is upon us.
>
> Let there be justice for all.
>
> Let there be peace for all.
>
> Let there be work, bread, water and salt for all.'

Can we apply Mandela's thoughts to ourselves in our own community here?

Escape from captivity

Are there chasms that divide us? Well, they aren't as great as those in South Africa, but we do have divisions, and jealousies and quarrels, and sometimes bullying. So we can ask that we can bridge the chasms that divide us.

The time to build? School is all about building, surely. Building knowledge, and learning. Building friendships as we grow together.

Justice for all? It's not easy to be fair to everyone, so we are right to say that we must try for fairness and equal treatment for everybody.

Peace for all? What better wish is there than for peace in our lives, our home, our school, our country and the world we share?

And what about Mandela's prayer for work, bread, water and salt? Every human being needs that – food and water for life, salt to make our food easy to eat, work for our self respect.

So let's repeat those sentences together.

‘The time for the healing of the wounds has come.

The moment to bridge the chasms that divide us has come.

The time to build is upon us.

Let there be justice for all.

Let there be peace for all.

Let there be work, bread, water and salt for all.'

☀ A prayer

Lord, we thank you for great leaders – for Moses and Mandela, and for all the others whom we admire and wish to follow. Give us the judgment to find good examples to follow, and the strength of character to hold to the principles that they teach us. Amen.

☀ A thought

We all need someone to look up to. The trick is to pick the right examples, and to be faithful to the principles they teach us.

Song suggestions

‘The wise may bring their learning,' *Come and Praise*, 64

‘Put your hand in the hand,' *Alleluya* 50

Optional follow up

Through history, many famous leaders spent some time as captives – some as prisoners of war, or political prisoners. Winston Churchill is just one example. See how many examples you can find. You could make an ‘Escape from captivity' wall display.